Dr Keith J. White is Director of Mill[...]
Ruth, he is responsible for the resid[...]
children who have experienced separation and loss. He is well
versed in the literature of child development and psychiatry. His first
degree was in English Literature, and he has researched residential
child care in Scotland and later in India. He is former President of
the UK Social Care Association and Chair of the National Council
of Voluntary Child Care Organisations. Currently, Keith is an
Associate Lecturer at Spurgeon's College and Visiting Lecturer in
Child Theology at the Malaysian Baptist Theological Seminary. He is
Chair of the Child Theology Movement, and Children Webmag, and
founder of the Christian Child Care Forum. Keith has worked for
two decades on a new edition of the Bible, *The Bible, Narrative and
Illustrated*, which was first published in 2006. His other publications
include *Entry Point* (with Prof. Haddon Willmer, WTL Publications,
2013), *In the Meantime* (WTL Publications, 2013), *Reflections on
Living with Children* (WLT Publications, 2010), *Caring for Deprived
Children* (as editor), *A Place for Us* (Editions 1 and 2), *In his Image,
The Art of Faith, Children and Social Exclusion* (editor) and *Celebrating
Children* (contributor) (Paternoster Press, 2003). He writes regular
columns in *Childrenwebmag* and *Outlook*. Keith has four grown-up
children and five grandchildren. He is currently writing a book on
Pandita Ramabai and is editing a number of child theology related
publications.

Barnabas
for
Children

Barnabas for Children® is a registered word mark and the logo is a registered device mark of The Bible Reading Fellowship.

Text copyright © Keith White 2008
The author asserts the moral right to be identified as the author of this work

Published by
The Bible Reading Fellowship
15 The Chambers, Vineyard
Abingdon OX14 3FE, United Kingdom
Tel: +44 (0)1865 319700
Email: enquiries@brf.org.uk
Website: www.brf.org.uk
BRF is a Registered Charity

ISBN 978 0 85746 075 2
First published 2008; this edition 2011
Reprinted 2014
10 9 8 7 6 5 4 3 2 1
All rights reserved

Acknowledgments
Unless otherwise stated, scripture quotations are taken from the Contemporary English Version of the Bible published by HarperCollins Publishers, copyright © 1991, 1992, 1995 American Bible Society.

Scripture quotations taken from The New Revised Standard Version of the Bible, Anglicized Edition, copyright © 1989, 1995 by the Division of Christian Education of the National Council of the Churches of Christ in the USA, are used by permission. All rights reserved.

Scripture quotations taken from the Holy Bible, New International Version, copyright © 1973, 1978, 1984 by International Bible Society, are used by permission of Hodder & Stoughton Publishers, a division of Hodder Headline Ltd. All rights reserved. 'NIV' is a registered trademark of International Bible Society. UK trademark number 1448790.

Scripture quotations from The Jerusalem Bible © 1966 by Darton, Longman & Todd Ltd and Doubleday & Company, Inc.

Scripture quotations marked (GNB) are from the Good News Bible published by The Bible Societies, copyright © 1966, 1971, 1976, 1992 American Bible Society.

Extracts from the Authorized Version of the Bible (The King James Bible), the rights in which are vested in the Crown, are reproduced by permission of the Crown's Patentee, Cambridge University Press.

Extract from *Offering the Gospel to Children* by Gretchen Wolff Pritchard, Cowley Publications, 1992. First appeared in *The Living Church*, October 14, 1990. Used by permission of Rowman & Littlefield Publishing Group, Maryland, USA.

p. 40: Diagram 'Human development reconfigured' taken from *The Logic of the Spirit* by James E. Loder (Jossey-Bass, 1998). Reproduced with permission of Global Rights Dept., John Wiley & Sons, Inc.

A catalogue record for this book is available from the British Library

Printed and bound by CPI Group (UK) Ltd, Croydon, CR0 4YY

THE GROWTH
OF LOVE

Understanding five essential elements of
child development

KEITH J WHITE

To Ruth, from whom I have learned
nearly all I know about love

CONTENTS

✤

FOREWORD

Many books have been written about child development, including heavyweight dissections of instincts and cultural conditioning, and treatises on educating the young mind and taming the wild child. Most show a lack of recognition that the tiniest baby has as many, and as deep, feelings as a mature adult, and is equally worthy of respect.

In *The Growth of Love*, Keith White talks about the unique and extraordinary community of Mill Grove, where each person is seen as 'made in the image of God' and therefore to be treated with love. White is not just a theoretician, he is also a hands-on practitioner. Although he has read extremely widely, he extrapolates from his own recollections of how the therapeutic community helps, and is enriched by, the young people who stay there. His wisdom, commitment and love shine through, and it is easy to place love at the meeting point between psychology and theology. When Christ said, 'Love thy neighbour as thyself', surely it was as much a statement of fact as an injunction, and it is clear from this book that it is the unhappy children who don't like themselves—who have not experienced security in a primary attachment relationship—who do not like others. At Mill Grove they learn that they have significance, that there are boundaries for behaviour which leave them free to explore, and that their trust will be honoured. In time, they come to understand that their value is immeasurable, and their ability to contribute to a community is great.

There are enormous riches of insight in White's writing: the strength in humility and vulnerability; the value of other cultures; the yardstick of humour and creativity to measure the return to psychological and spiritual health; and most importantly, the truly life-giving value of love, both given and received. Every page of this book is worth reading: you will nod in recognition, or hold your breath in revelation.

Sir Richard Bowlby, President of the Centre for Child Mental Health, London

INTRODUCTION

This book has been gestating for a period of 20 years of more—so long that in the process it has been trailed and prefigured in many lectures, papers and articles in different parts of the world.[1] The raw material from which it draws is the daily practical experience of living alongside children and young people at Mill Grove. The rest is a reflection on this life together using mainly, though not exclusively, psycho-social theory and theology.

Since 1976 my wife Ruth and I have lived with hurting children and young people, and, as we have tried to understand their stories, resilience, strengths, needs and growth, the themes about which I am writing have gradually emerged.

As I have studied the way love grows, from the perspectives of both psycho-social theory and theology, I have been drawn to the conclusion that much of their wisdom and many of their core insights are mutually enriching. So you can read this book as an endeavour not only to link the two but also to see if it is possible to arrive at a new place of understanding enlightened by each of them. Significantly, both are informed by encounters with the realities of human life and suffering and have been forged in the crucible of experience.

SOME SOURCES OF MATERIAL AND INSPIRATION

Others, of course, have sought to work at this interface before me, and I would like to acknowledge some of those who have helped to light the way for me. One is Dr Frank Lake, the founder of the Clinical Theology Movement. His major work, *Clinical Theology*, is subtitled 'A theological and psychological basis to clinical and pastoral care'.[2] My wife Ruth studied Clinical Theology under Frank's daughter Janet, and his attempted integration with all its challenges and unresolved dilemmas is still a formative influence on our life and work. Then there is the work of Bruce Reed (whom I came to know as a friend), notably *The Dynamics of Religion*.[3] This represents a lifetime of analysis of personal and group dynamics, with particular reference to creative regression and its place in wholeness and growth, drawing widely from psychoanalytic and therapeutic literature as well as a rich experience of the Jewish and Christian scriptures.

James Loder, in *The Logic of the Spirit*,[4] has provided some creative insights into how theology and models of human development might engage with each other. He is prepared to offer a completely different starting point from that of the prevailing psycho-social theory and his argument deserves careful reflection and study by Christians who sense that something important is missing from contemporary theories of child development.

The books of the Swiss psychiatrist Paul Tournier provided wonderful companionship during the 1970s. We have most of his books, including *The Meaning of Persons*[5] and *A Place for You*,[6] and have drawn from both his wisdom and his humble approach. Like Lake, Loder and Reed, his life's work is an attempt to integrate his Christian faith with his professional (in his case, psychiatric) training.

I read R.S. Lee's *Freud and Christianity*[7] as a research graduate. Lee was a pioneer indicating some of the contours of the road before those of us travelling in these two related fields. Victor Frankl, notably *Man's Search for Meaning: an Introduction to Logotherapy*,[8] and Carl Jung, particularly *Modern Man in Search of a Soul*,[9] were early mentors. In different ways they sought to span the worlds of faith (spirituality) and psychoanalytic theory. A more recent British writer committed to this task of integration is Roger Hurding, *Roots and Shoots*.[10]

All these writers were thinking primarily about adults, even if they saw many of the seeds of the adults' personalities, identities and relationships in their past childhood experiences. One of the challenges less often attempted is some form of integration that focuses on children and young people.

In my reading of literature from different parts of the world, I have often found some of the deepest connections in the works of poets and novelists, who may not have used technical terms but have seen into the human soul with clarity and discovered that no one discipline is adequate to describe its riches, potential and depths. It is only since I have been engaged in Child Theology that, in rereading some of my favourite writers, such as Dostoevsky, I have realized how important children are to their understanding of the world, life and death.

This far from exhaustive list indicates the range and variety of those who have operated somewhere along this intersection between the history of psycho-social theory and theology. I am indebted to them and to many others who have been willing to share their questions, doubts and ideas so openly.

While mulling over the contents of this book over the years, I have also been working on a new edition of the Bible (*The Bible, Narrative and Illustrated*), and this process has been a challenging and informative resource throughout. It has helped me to work on the full canon of scripture with care, and I have become increasingly convinced that Christians alongside children are often unaware of the scale and depth of the resources available to them in this remarkable library of 66 books.

MAKING CONNECTIONS

The reason I have chosen the five words that are at the core of this book (security, boundaries, significance, community and creativity) rather than many suggested alternatives is that they serve best, in my view, to connect these two fields of operation and enquiry. They enable committed people in either discipline to bring what they know into contact with those coming from a different perspective, without compromise on the one hand and without imperialism on the other. None of the five words is the copyright or exclusive property of anyone. A fuller explanation is given in Chapter Two.

If you ask me which—either psycho-social theory or theology—is the dominant partner, I can honestly say that I will never know. My continuous journey of discovery informed by reflection on practice, and aided by equally continuous reading and discussion in theology and psycho-social theory, has provided a wide-ranging conversation comprising many reciprocal insights and discoveries. Again and again, my reading of the scriptures has been enlightened by the works of pioneers in the field of child welfare, and likewise my study of how children develop has been enriched and guided by the timeless insights of the scriptures.

One of the most practical examples of such an insight concerns the relationship between little children and the 'kingdom of heaven'. Jesus taught that they were inextricably linked: to enter the kingdom, adults needed to change and become like little children (see Matthew 18:3). In 1999, I began tentatively to explore the nature and possible meanings of this relationship, and one of the simplest ways of doing so was to apply what I knew about the kingdom of heaven to children and vice versa. When theologians talk of this kingdom as being 'now' and 'not yet', I find it a very apt and practical description of childhood (see Chapter Two for further explanation of this idea). In fact, you could see any imbalance between the 'now' and the 'not yet' as leading to problems in understanding and relating to children. Likewise, keeping a child in mind—and acknowledging that 'now' and 'not yet' apply equally to adults—might help to ensure that the kingdom of heaven does not become trapped in the adult discourses of politics, size, power and territory.[11]

My primary reason for this work has been not so much the attempt to find an academic synthesis and new theoretical models as the desire to understand better the lives, struggles, growth and development of particular children and families. Daily life has provided the context in which this interaction has taken place, so I owe the children and young people among whom I live a debt of gratitude: it is their resilience and honesty that have inspired and informed my journey of discovery.

REIMAGINING PARENTHOOD

One of the reasons I am writing this book is my conviction that 'parenting' is not restricted to the nuclear family of those adults immediately related to the child. Love's growth is not confined to the quality of these biological relationships alone, although they are of great importance. In my view, parenting is a responsibility and gift of everyone directly or indirectly involved in a child's life, whether parents, family, neighbourhood, school or society. I likewise resist any tendency to equate 'care' with home, religion with church (or place of worship), and education with school. It seems to me that if we are to understand the growth of love in a child, we need to see that the process is likely to involve and transcend any of these groups as it engages and interweaves with each of them.

Of course, this is hardly an original view of things, even if we do need reminding of its long history. The phrase 'it takes a village to parent' has become well known in recent years. There are many suggested sources for this quotation, and I am happy to accept that it represents much of the wisdom from around the world. As it happens, I have beside me, as I write, the book by Hillary Clinton, *It Takes a Village*,[12] in which she develops the idea drawing from her unusually extensive experience.

One of the arguments of my book is that it takes a village (or some equivalent) for love to grow within and between human beings. I use the term 'village' metaphorically, so what I write is equally applicable to urban and rural life. Likewise, when speaking of 'villagers', I am imagining all of us to be members of what is sometimes thought of as a global village. The village is not, of course, the instrument of love's growing. Love is not produced in this functional sort of way. It would be more accurate to say that individuals grow within community. This leads me to a point I want to make clearly and sensitively at the beginning of this book: the growth of love is not completely dependent on only one strand of a child's life and experience, or limited to one or two significant adults at a particular stage of life.

This is of critical importance not only to my argument but also to all of us, whatever roles or tasks we have in the global village. We may or may not be biological parents. We may or may not be teachers or people engaged alongside children in the Christian community. Yet we all have a part to play in creating the environment in which love can thrive. To look at it another way, we need not despair if we feel (or even know) that we have failed in our responsibilities towards a particular child. We are not alone, and this failure, real or imagined, is not the end of the story.

Let me describe an experience I had in Switzerland, as a way of explaining what I mean by this broad and inclusive understanding of parenting, represented by the words 'village' and 'villagers'. It was a mid-morning in the Easter holidays, and I was with some of the family of Mill Grove, driving through a Swiss village between Heiden and Teufen. As providence would have it, the village was Trogen, site of the famous Pestalozzi Children's Village. Three kindergarten-age children carrying satchels came up to the kerb on our right where there was a road crossing.

We slowed down until our car came to a halt. They skipped across the road and continued their walk home from school. It was an unremarkable event in the sense that the scene is replicated all over rural Switzerland every day, so why was it so memorable for us? Quite simply because, although there were no adults to be seen, the children obviously felt safe and were completely at ease.

It is difficult to think of a place in the UK where this would have happened, outside the Western Isles of Scotland and a few equally remote rural areas. Everywhere else, it would have been considered gross negligence on the part of the parents or the kindergarten. Who was protecting these little children against physical dangers, strangers and paedophiles? The answer, of course, is that *we* were. By virtue of driving into the area, we had become 'villagers'—part of the village that was raising these children—and immediately our awareness was heightened. We looked behind as we moved off to make sure they were safe and kept our eyes open for other youngsters as we drove through other villages.

How is it that in one country this is the norm while in another it is virtually unthinkable? I have pondered this long and hard and have come to the conclusion that it is something that goes right to the heart of culture and tradition. In Switzerland there is a very different sense of community (*gemeinde*) from what we understand by the word in English. The Gemeinde (that is, the local authority) will inspect your house each year and, in the case of wooden farmhouses, will pay particular attention to the state of the chimney. The same Gemeinde will take responsibility for its citizens throughout their lives, and those who serve the Gemeinde will generally do so with a sense of diligence or pride. (I am referring here to the teachers, postal and transport workers, and those who tend the parks and footpaths.) The evidence is to be seen in the general upkeep of the village, but everyone has a part to play.

I am led to wonder whether the comparative tidiness and absence of litter in Switzerland is socially significant and can help us here. It seems to me to represent some ownership of responsibility for the public spaces and environment of which the citizens are part, or through which they pass. There does not seem to be the same working distinction—made largely unconsciously, in my view—between 'my personal space' for which I accept responsibility and that I like to see clean and tidy, and 'the outside world' (village) for which I take no responsibility and possibly don't even notice.

In reality, there are problems associated with societies like Japan and Switzerland that have tight-knit communal bonds—they are not utopias, either for adults or for children—but as an ideal type I believe that a child-friendly society will tend to celebrate communal relationships alongside individual privacy. If there were absolute family or personal privacy in every area of life, then there would be neither village nor villager. Parenting of the sort that I am advocating would be impossible.

I quote this example because it was in Switzerland that I saw the truth of what it really meant to become part of the village that parents. We were in no way related to those kindergarten children, biologically or culturally, but they accepted us as part of the social canopy in which they felt safe. One of the key elements of that canopy is that it is made up of a number of different threads and textures. For this reason, it is important for every reader to understand that I am not proposing one type of intervention, theory or model of care.

Perhaps we tend to be allured by a system or theory that offers a quick fix. Perhaps we believe that we can chart outcomes in relation to input. That may be true of the production of baked beans but it will simply never do when it comes to the growth of love. So this book is not about a particular method or theory. It is about identifying the qualities of the psychological, social and physical landscape in which children may best thrive, and it is written in the belief that we all have a part to play in the construction and nurture of that environment.

JOHN BOWLBY

A final comment before we start: I harboured the desire for many years that this book would be meticulously researched and perhaps even, in a very limited way, a successor of sorts to John Bowlby's great, groundbreaking work, *Maternal Care and Mental Health*,[13] which became better known in the summary, *Child Care and the Growth of Love*.[14] Bowlby rarely uses the word 'love' in either book, apart from the title in the second, and in research it is a difficult word to define or measure, but when he talks of 'mother-love'[15] there is little doubt about what he means: 'a warm, intimate and continuous relationship with his mother... in which both find satisfaction and enjoyment'.[16]

Often, the meaning he has in mind is evident when he describes the opposite: 'superficial relationships; no real feeling—no capacity to care for people or to make true friends; an inaccessibility, exasperating to those trying to help; no emotional response to situations where it is normal—a curious lack of concern; deceit and evasion, often pointless; stealing...'.[17] This list is useful as a starting point for describing some of the attributes of love—that is the giving and receiving of affection, promises, tenderness, and the capacity for, and willingness to, sacrifice one's own comfort for the sake of another.

There is little doubt in my mind that whatever John Bowlby would have made of this book, he would recognize the same basic understanding of what love entails and share an acute concern about the potential effects of its absence. He drew from experience and research involving children who had been separated from their parents for health or social reasons, and that is the source of my own evidence and information. We both write with the conviction of those who realize that poverty of love is one of the worst forms of deprivation on earth.

It will quickly become apparent, however, that although this book draws heavily from Bowlby and his successors, it is not as carefully researched as their material. In fact, I have found myself snatching odd moments in a busy winter schedule, and what follows is largely dependent on memories and recollections rather than reading and research. The book is written in the heat and under the pressure of daily life and practice. Because it comes from the crucible of life among children and young people, I hope you will receive it in that spirit.

❖

Chapter One

THE PLACE WHERE WE STARTED

We shall not cease from exploration
And the end of all our exploring
Will be to arrive where we started
And know the place for the first time.

T.S. Eliot, 'Little Gidding', *Four Quartets*

On 20 November 1899, while Victoria was still Queen of England and Empress of India, my grandfather Herbert White was moved with compassion by the plight of an eight-year-old motherless girl called Rosie. He arranged for a female Sunday school teacher in his church to care for Rosie in the little flat above the shop where she worked in the east of London. That was where and how 'Mill Grove' started.

Mill Grove is the name given to two large houses situated in South Woodford, London. They are both Victorian, although one looks a lot older than the other. They are the original buildings but have been adapted over the years. You will find the neighbourhood on the Central Line of the London Underground, east of Stratford and Leyton.

Over the years after Rosie was taken in, more children were cared for in larger accommodation, with a maximum of 60 at any one time. Had you visited the place in the 1920s, it would perhaps have reminded you of a boarding school, with uniforms, 'houses', long scrubbed white tables and wooden forms for meals, and lots of sports competitions.

In the 1950s it would have seemed like a children's home, but by the 1970s there was a growing awareness that it had become quite unlike anything else. This is why the name Mill Grove was chosen—as a way of allowing the place to develop in its own way rather than having predetermined labels attached to it.[1]

Since 1901 it has been the home of a biologically related family descended from Herbert White. It is also the home of children and, more recently, families who for whatever reason cannot live in their own homes. As the community of those living here has mushroomed, Mill Grove has become the hub of a worldwide extended family, and it is a place where neighbours know they can come for support and practical help. There is lots of informal contact with local people of all ages, as well as a pre-school nursery, a toddler group, a school for children with cerebral palsy, and various local groups that use the premises.

Since 1931 Mill Grove has been an interdenominational Christian charity with a board of trustees, and it has a threefold purpose: to care for children in need, to seek to introduce them by example and word to God's love as revealed uniquely in Jesus Christ, and to rely on God alone to meet all the needs that arise.[2]

Residential communities, notably those called communes, often set out to pursue a particular form or way of living. By way of contrast, Mill Grove has evolved as it has responded to the needs of others rather than as the outcome of a master plan or vision. In some important respects, it is an unintentional extended family or residential community. Part of what we do is registered as a 'children's home' for practical purposes,[3] but those whose roots are in Africa and Asia see it as much more typical of an extended family. Only last week, a visitor from Uganda told me while we were chatting at the kitchen sink that it felt just like home. Some who have reflected theologically see it as a way of 'being church'.[4]

Although the dynamics and nature of Mill Grove have been shaped in the course of its mission and by its response to the needs of particular children and families, there has also been sustained reflection on how we live together. We have studied and learned from much writing about, and practical experience of, residential communities.[5] Alternative living requires not only conviction and determination but also careful monitoring and analysis.

When analysed, Mill Grove is rather unusual in that it comprises both a biological family and a residential community with patterns of life distinct from, and a range of activities some way beyond, those of more ordinary families and households. So while those who are part of this 'family' enjoy life together without undue need for definitions and categorization, others remain puzzled by what it is and how it should be classified.[6]

Since 1899, over 1200 children have lived at Mill Grove and probably an even greater number have been supported through its life and work. All things being equal, it might have grown into a national organization by now, but it has resisted the usual growth and publicity. Perhaps that is how and why it has become such a radical alternative community where there is lifelong commitment to every child in the name of Jesus.

A PARADOX

I was born at Mill Grove and have lived here most of my life. The place in which I am writing the major part of this book was the bedroom of my grandparents, where I sat on their bed and opened a present from them on my fifth birthday and where I put a little posy of flowers on my grandfather's coffin. Apart from about ten years away, first as a student and then in the early years of our married life, this has been my home. The large houses and garden are in an unexceptional neighbourhood and suburb of London. It is no modern-day garden of Eden! As I look out of the window I can see the busy intersection between the M11 motorway and the North Circular road. There is a power pylon dominating the horizon and factories on two sides of our garden.

For over a century this has been my family home (it is now five generations that have been involved), and we have opened the doors of our home and hearts to children and young people who have been unable to live with their own families. Some of these children were told before they came that it was an awful place, to which they were being sent because they were naughty, and generations of social workers have dedicated their practice to keeping children out of places like Mill Grove, which they see as a last resort.[7]

If you live in a place for as long as I have lived here, you become acutely aware of its besetting difficulties, weaknesses and imperfections. You realize that it could be much better given more resources, wisdom and training. You recognize the tensions; the unresolved dilemmas and contradictions. You know that all who have been there in the role of caring adults have had more than their fair share of needs and problems. You have heard anguished, angry outbursts and observed the withdrawn behaviour of children who feel they have been unheard or poorly served by the community.

Mill Grove exists because there is hurt, separation, loss and cruelty in the lives of children, and children have come mostly because others have sent them here, not because they have chosen to come. This has changed in recent years but in general it is true—and yet, in and through all this, two notable things continue to happen.

First, those who come to experience the place as visitors often say that they find a deep sense of spirituality and peace. These are not occasional comments, but an almost universal reaction. I recall one youngster coming home after years away. He was hungry and feeling rejected yet again. We were chatting as he consumed a substantial meal, when he suddenly paused and said, 'That's it! That's what I had forgotten about this place—the peace.' It is that very word that I have heard again and again. Others have used the word 'spirituality'. When I have prodded them to defend and explain what they mean, they have never once withdrawn what they have said despite my challenges.

On the occasion of our centenary service in May 2000, the extended family that had gathered from all over the world was invited to sing Albert Mallotte's setting of the Lord's Prayer. As people streamed forward, a bishop and a professor of medicine, who were sitting in the front row absorbing the scene, both remarked to me that it was like a 'foretaste of heaven'. That was perhaps understandable because it was a remarkable and unforgettable experience for us all, far removed from the ordinary grind of daily life, but there are also those who have found a glimpse of heaven amid the sheer plod and struggles of each day.

Here is part of a recent letter:

Thank you for welcoming us to Mill Grove. It is difficult to put into words what we all felt while we were there, but we continue to talk about our visit and try to describe it to our friends. Each of us ended up by saying something like 'This place is bizarre' ... But it was admiration... I know that we saw Jesus at work.

A second remarkable thing is more directly linked to the theme of this book. As we have listened to the stories of those who have lived here over the past decades, we have begun to discover that love has grown in and between them while they were living here, and has continued now that they are dispersed. Despite all the pressures, limitations and difficulties, it has been a place where love has grown.

Here is part of a letter written by the daughter of someone who came to live at Mill Grove as a young girl in 1944. The grandmother of the letter writer had been unable to care for her children, which is why they came to Mill Grove. At the end of the grandmother's life, there was reconciliation:

That was a picture of forgiveness that will never leave me; part of a legacy that began when God provided a home for the girls when they had none. Our extended family is deeply aware of the instrument of love that Mill

Grove has been and the impact of so many obedient and godly people in God's plan... I truly believe that through the love of the White family the girls were able to offer grace and forgiveness to Granny, and thwart the Enemy's plan to see the perpetuation of evil and bitterness.

Here are the words written in a Christmas card by the mother of one of the children we have helped over several years, a child who is with us today as he always is on a Sunday:

So hard to put into words what is inside and exactly how I feel. But I'll try. You have become very dear to us. And Mill Grove has provided and given so much in so many different ways. I'm thankful for the love and for the sense of belonging, the acceptance, love, time, commitment you show. We love you dearly.

Recently I was present at the funeral of a woman who had married one of the boys who used to live at Mill Grove. Their marriage, their family life as parents and grandparents, their church engagement and friendships all spoke of love, and the bereavement of a member of the Mill Grove family had stirred memories around the world. In South Africa, Australasia and North America there were those who had grown up with him and spoke of him as a brother, whom they still loved 40 years after having lived together.

I cannot say how many who have lived at Mill Grove have found this sort of experience to be true through the generations, but in the lives of many I have known over the years, love has grown. One of the things I try to do in what follows is to identify and describe some of the factors that may have contributed to and nourished that process, but this book is not a research study using statistics or describing techniques.[8]

If Mill Grove were planned, purpose-driven, not to say professional, then we might be tempted to describe our methods and advocate them as a model to be copied elsewhere. Because we are so aware of the limitations, that way is thankfully not open to us.

As youngsters have described and told their stories again and again, we have tried to piece together the varied, angular and precarious processes by which love grows.[9] I have become aware of the elements that are described repeatedly in these stories, like recurring motifs, and in the process I have been struck by how often these motifs replicate the themes not only at the heart of the biblical story and stories, but also in the observations of the psychotherapists and analysts.

A WAY OF LIFE

It may be useful for you to have a little background information about the context of my life and work at Mill Grove. Let me summarize its most important characteristics by using the five words listed in the Introduction, which provide the structure for this book.

First, Mill Grove has been a place of permanence and *security*. It has remained where it began. It has not changed location, address, telephone number, family or mission. It is a bit like a rock that those who knew it as children can rely on to be there, unshakeable and immovable. They assume that it always will be there. A letter I have beside me, which arrived a day or two ago, from another 'former boy' who had recently lost his wife, says, 'Thank you for your support and prayers. It means so much to know that you are there...' A moment's reflection reveals how significant and unique this is. There have been many other causes that started in the UK in the 19th century concerned with the care of orphans and destitute children. The names continue but the nature of their operation has changed dramatically. In many cases the adults who used to care for the children, and the places where the children were cared for, have gone.

By contrast, Mill Grove is marked by a commitment which means that no leader of the community has ever moved away or been intentionally unavailable should one of the family be in need. It is simply 'there' and can be taken for granted, in the very best sense, by the children and former children. It is not that the place has remained impervious to changes in culture and technology or, for that matter, theory. It has, like any organism, adapted to changing conditions and with changing times, but its calling is to provide a similar function to some of the special sacred places in the world religions: they are there so that, wherever you are, you have the security of knowing your bearings.

Of course, we cannot predict or shape the future in any reliable way so I do not know what the future of Mill Grove will be, but, a century after its beginnings, it remains a place that is 'there', and in any planning the issue of security will be the prime consideration.

Secondly, Mill Grove has provided a number of *boundaries* for the children who have become part of the family. One of the common characteristics of their lives before coming to Mill Grove is a sense of unreliability, unpredictability and even chaos. When they arrive, they begin to discover a shape and form to each day, week, month and year. Although there is much that is unexpected and spontaneous, whether by way of celebration or crisis, the family has always tried to function in a way that is predictable and reliable. Patterns of life have provided a context for growth and development.

Looking back, perhaps these boundaries were more pronounced than those in ordinary families of the time, but it meant that the children knew where they were. It was possible to anticipate what would happen and therefore to plan accordingly. Moral and social boundaries were lived out by the adults as far as they could in line with what they understood to be God's will. The marriage covenant of the three couples who have led the community has been sacred in each case.

We have a good deal of space, and over the years we have tried to organize the way it is used to provide secure privacy for members of the family, opportunities and frameworks for shared living, and a sensitive, welcoming yet discerning relationship with the outside world. We have discovered the truth that 'good fences make good neighbours'.[10]

Thirdly, Mill Grove has been a place where everyone who lives there is known by name. Each child has mattered as an individual, has been known personally, and has known that there would be people who would never forget them as long as they lived. The word used in the book for this is *significance*. It is not just about policies and rights, although these have their place. It goes deeper than that. Every person needs to know that there is someone else on earth who cares about them enough to be there for them (to hold them in their hearts) whatever happens—someone who matters to them and will receive their affection and honour their trust. It is a two-way process, or 'inter-subjectivity', that is the essence of what we mean by the word 'relationship'.

One of my childhood memories is of sitting on the carpet beside the table where my grandmother was writing with her Conway Stewart fountain pen. For some reason, I have always been inordinately fond of fountain pens, so I recall the scene vividly. She was writing letters to members of the Mill Grove family around the world, and each day we would remember family members by name in our prayers.[11]

Although the family is a large one by conventional standards, it is small enough for every former child to have been known as an individual. I have been present when people have come back 60 or even 70 years after living at Mill Grove, to be welcomed by my parents or relatives with a warm embrace. Over cups of tea there has been a seemingly never-ending sequence of stories of times shared together, and the names and stories have been handed down so that the next generation is part of the process of remembering and valuing each person by name. To my knowledge, there has never been a person who has returned without being immediately recognized and welcomed (without recourse to records, files and photos).

The fourth characteristic is a sense of belonging and *community* that goes beyond the walls of Mill Grove. The residential community belongs to a neighbourhood, to the local and wider Christian community, and has grown into an international family of several generations. There are many layers to the links, with interlocking groups and associations. In this way, children find that, far from being separated and isolated from the rest of the world, they are encouraged to be in touch with social groups so that they can join them should they choose to do so.[12] Our holiday home in North Wales likewise links the children into another set of relationships and a wholly different community with its own language. Our global personal connections mean that we regularly have people from different continents visiting and coming to stay with us. So, in a number of simple ways, the life of the family is anything but self-contained and inward-looking.

Finally, there is a lot of *creativity*. I hope the meaning of this will become apparent as the book proceeds, but suffice it to say at this stage that it includes enjoying and valuing fun, games, play and improvisation. Part of the prevailing ethos is that laughter and jokes, and the enjoyment of being and playing together, are right at the heart of things. Such an ethos cannot be programmed into a place: it is part of its very being and nature. My grandfather and father are remembered for their interest in sport, and a fondness for puns and jokes seems to be part of the family's genes. If you look at any issue of *Links*, the newsletter,[13] it quickly becomes apparent that this is a place where play and exploration are the stuff of life together.

Creativity thrives on and generates new experiences, individual and shared, even in familiar surroundings, and context and resources are important elements in the facilitation of play. It is not about mechanical provision of crayons or toys with an expectation of what is to be produced, but more like introducing children to settings where, through relationships, imagination and serendipities, something unexpected is discovered or shaped. Again, the house in North Wales is a great blessing: not only is it a passport to the natural adventure playground of Snowdonia, but it also has a resource room full of materials, information and equipment to aid every kind of creativity.

It is often easier to define something by saying what it is not. In the Introduction, I noted how John Bowlby, for example, described the opposite of love. So it may be helpful to say that Mill Grove is not a place of mechanical routine, grey walls and clothes, rotas and an institutionalized way of living, with the members of the community functioning like cogs in a machine. If you are thinking historically, it could be seen as the very opposite of a workhouse or asylum. To be present at just one birthday party would dispel any lingering doubts about that.

Perhaps it is helpful to emphasize the fact that although Mill Grove seeks to provide a safe therapeutic environment in which children can discover acceptance and healing, this context is not dominated by treatment regimes and techniques. The overriding ethos is that of a family sensitive to and in tune with seasons and patterns of life. The belief is that, through these seasons and processes, children (as individuals and as members of a group) will be helped to discover that they are creators and creative, their contributions valued and valuable—that they matter and that they count. Play is one of the key elements of the whole process and way of life.

This brief summary is not intended to disguise the reality that some of the children who have lived here have always felt insecure, insignificant (lacking self-esteem) and anxious. Rather, it is an attempt to describe the beliefs and values that are the very stuff of the place. Those values explain why it is still here and why it is still very precious to many people of different generations. Despite its imperfections, it has provided a 'good enough' context, in and through which many have found that they can begin to be able to give and receive love. Sometimes this has only been possible after a number of mistakes and misguided attempts.

I hope this short and honest overview will encourage and provide hope to readers: if people maintain connections with children and young people, whatever their limitations, there is always hope that love will be kindled and come alive, even amid the unlikeliest of stories and circumstances. Love does not require the equivalent of an emotional and psychological greenhouse in order to thrive.

In the Introduction, I argued for an understanding of parenting congruent with the traditional wisdom that it takes a village to parent. In case there is any doubt about it, I would like to emphasize the fact that Mill Grove is not a self-sufficient 'village' or 'family' in which all the resources for the growth of love are to be found—very much the reverse, in fact. As I have tried to show, it has always recognized that it is but one part of the context of the life of children. It seeks to tap into other networks and caring systems, so schools and churches, friends, clubs and neighbours are all highly valued. Bonds and attachments with the child's own family and roots have been preserved and nurtured where possible and desirable.

We do not seek to offer the sort of environment typical of 'total institutions'—like, say, a monastery or a prison—in which the whole of a person's life can be lived during the time they remain there. This has helped me to see the way in which the different elements and pieces of a child's life may together contribute to the context in which love can grow. Mill Grove is part of a village. For some children it has functioned like a self-contained womb for a period in their lives; for others it has been much more like a temporary resting place or launchpad. What it seeks to do is to be there for each child, to offer what that child most needs and desires, and to receive what that child may wish to give.

You will have gathered by now that it is not possible to say exactly how Mill Grove has helped each child: individual teachers, families, neighbours, friends and Sunday school teachers have all had their part to play. This book does not seek to encourage readers to become or create all-round environments for every child, sufficient and entire in themselves, but to play an appropriate part in parenting.

SUMMARY

It is the longevity of a community based in the same place, with its sustained relationships, that has provided me with such unique source material for this book. If connections with the children had ceased at the moment they left Mill Grove or, for that matter, a few years afterwards, I guess we would have concluded that there was sometimes little evidence of the shoots, buds or blossoms of love. But from a vantage point that enables me to scan whole lifetimes and to trace what happens in the next generation or two, I am able to see sustained and remarkable evidence of love given and received by those who had experienced traumas, loss and abuse at crucial times of their lives.

Some see Mill Grove as a very special place—a respected model of Christian residential care for children and families. It is as if it were put on a modest pedestal, setting it apart from ordinary families and communities, and therefore it is assumed that it cannot be replicated. As it happens, I don't think that any family can be replicated or cloned: the individuality and diversity of families, whether around us or in the Bible, are more striking than anything that they have in common.[14]

Whatever conclusions people draw about Mill Grove, it has quietly tried, over the decades, to live as a community by simple truths, committed to well-tried principles and wisdom. For this reason, it exemplifies what is happening, largely unsung, in many families, nuclear and extended, around the world. Mill Grove could be any family if that family is allowed to grow and develop through the generations, living in the same place and committed to the same vision.

The story, of course, continues to unfold as I write. In fact, it has been continuing with such vigour and making such demands as I have been working on this book that I have often wondered about my priorities. No doubt there will be surprises ahead, including our fair share of disappointments, but they will only help us to learn a little more about human potential and resilience, frailty and blindness, and perhaps make us a little wiser.

This is the place where I started, and after 60 years I am coming to know certain aspects of the place for the first time. That is why it seemed worth trying to encapsulate a little of this journey of discovery in a book.

✥

Chapter Two

FIVE-FINGER EXERCISE ON A FOUR-LETTER WORD

Love is kind and patient... Love is always supportive, loyal, hopeful, and trusting. Love never fails!

1 Corinthians 13:4, 7–8

I didn't plan to end up with five motifs for this book: that's just the way things turned out. I have never seen a way of reducing the number and, despite lots of encouragement, neither have I been convinced that there should be more. So it is serendipitous that we have the same number of motifs as most people have fingers on one hand—and that's where the title of this chapter comes from.

THE FIVE THEMES

The reason I have chosen the words security, boundaries, significance, community and creativity for the five motifs or themes is to enable an interplay and, in some cases, integration between different perspectives and traditions. The words are accessible to ordinary people and used in common parlance while at the same time resonating with theology and child development theory. I have tested them out in a variety of groups around the world—some academics, some care workers, some secular and professional, others theological and several where there has been a mixture of people with different approaches.

Whatever we might say about the merits or limitations of the five themes, many students and listeners have found that they provide a framework which enables some level of conversation between the discourses of everyday life, theology and child development theory. For some reason they are memorable. Parents, teachers, and social workers have recited to me the names of the five themes years after first hearing them, and told me how important they were to their way of understanding children, learning and care.

Such people are committed to doing their best to create a social, moral, physical, emotional, intellectual and spiritual environment in which children can thrive, and these five words describe what they recognize as essential elements of the process. The themes resonate with and represent in some form the wealth of historical and cultural experience informing our view of what makes the best conditions for the survival and growth of children. The United Nations Convention on the Rights of the Child[1] seeks to base its list of rights on the aggregate wisdom and understanding of just this fund of knowledge. We must be careful, however, to avoid the implication that the right conditions will always guarantee survival and growth. This would, among other things, deny the place of individual agency, resilience and God's grace.

The words for the five themes chime equally well with theological and child development perspectives. They are neither simply external (sociological) nor merely intrapersonal (psychological); they include these standpoints as well as the interpersonal. They aim at connecting the two disciplines of theology and child development. This means that they do not assume that a particular perspective is the more important one, or that there is one size that fits all children or all cultures and contexts. The environment we seek to construct or, if we leave things as they are, to accept as the context for childhood, must do justice to the tension between the 'here-and-now' and the 'not yet' of childhood. It will value the creative tension between the two interwoven modes of existence—on the one hand, play, daydreaming and messing about, which are primarily located in the present, and, on the other, education and nurture, which tend to look ahead.

All the time, we must be alert to the fact that it is perilously easy to intervene in children's lives, whether as individual parents or as organizations and states, in what we believe to be their best (future) interests—doing things to them and for them—only to discover that we have undermined the very elements that we seek to preserve and encourage. It is in the playgrounds and playtimes, the nooks and crannies, the dreams, and the spaces between lessons and sessions that some of the most important growth of self-esteem, community and creativity emerges. Even if we doubt this—and the current trend seems to stress preparation for adult roles and organized activity (whether in schools or families)—it makes sense to have some periods of gestation between lessons and experiments.

So these five themes do not constitute a manual of how to ensure the most effective transition from childhood to adulthood, immaturity to maturity. They represent, rather, an attempt to be true to the creative tensions inherent in childhood between the individual and the collective, the now and the not yet, the planned and the unplanned, the conscious and the unconscious, the functional and the spontaneous, the latent and the manifest, and between the forces of life and death. As we will see in Chapter Eight, these tensions exist in various shapes and forms throughout life.

The five words are open, fluid and expansive. Human experience, individual and collective, does not come neatly packaged, and human development is anything but linear, predictable and programmed. The contexts for human growth come in any number of different combinations. So this book is rooted in and seeks to describe real life and experience—making it clear that people have real, practical choices to make.

REFLECTING ON 'STAGES OF GROWTH'

Some people have asked whether the five motifs can be used interchangeably and in any order or whether they are equivalent to the stages of growth that some theoreticians suggest. Are they, for example, a variation on Erikson's stages of growth, starting with trust and moving towards identity? Let me say that I did not intend them to be so, and they are certainly not another version of Maslow's very popular (and, in my view, very questionable) 'hierarchy of needs'.

That said, I am quite sure that *security* is the most fundamental, basic and primal of the themes. It is of a different logical order to the others. We can just about conceive of some sort of human development without community (however stunted it might be), but if there is no security then human growth ceases. Survival, defence, freezing, denial, subterfuge and splitting are the predominant mechanisms in such a sad situation, and they leave little or no room for exploration, wistfulness and spontaneous experiments, conversation, games, dances and play, which are the stuff of human development. That is why I always start with security.

However, it has been pointed out to me by my dear friend and colleague Dr Jo-Joy Wright, a child psychologist, that there is a progression inherent in the five themes, even if it does not constitute a systematized version of stages of growth.[2] Thus life begins with the fundamental longing for security. On this, psycho-social theories and theology agree. Children need to experience the most basic safety that allows them to pause without fear—to eat, to laugh and to cry. Dr Wright, like me, would always place security at the beginning of any process.

Boundaries follow. Of course, they are part of the very process of creating and experiencing security, but in the young child it is patterns, structures and predictability that are so vital in growth. If the world is unpredictable and unreliable, there is little scope for the experimentation that development requires.

Significance, which (as we will see) embraces self-esteem and identity, emerges from this secure and predictable context, and goes hand in hand with the development of a sense of belonging to a wider *community* than the nuclear or extended family household. And although *creativity* is part of the process all through, it is also a byproduct. Children are born with imagination, as little makers or creators, and, given the right conditions, this creativity of infinite varieties will flourish.

Jo-Joy Wright continues to develop this idea with imagination and skill. One way she does so is to relate the five themes in order to the three resilience factors described by Grotberg: 'I am; I can; I have'. She then suggests a way of seeing how we can help children in each of these stages, described thus: 'Held, Heard and Healing'.[3]

While acknowledging and rejoicing in this possible logic in the ordering of the themes, I would like to stress that my experience is of any number of permutations in the lives of the children and young people that I have sought to know and help. I recall John Bowlby saying the same thing when asked about the stages or hurdles to growth in a seminar in Edinburgh. He said that different children faced and overcame them in different sequences. So care must be taken if the motifs are thought to represent a sequence.

I try to draw out practical applications as I proceed through the book, but there is one that overshadows all others: in our parenting, teaching, social work or child ministry, we need to get some idea of whether or not a child is experiencing security before deciding how best to intervene. I am reluctantly drawn to the conclusion that much of the business and busyness that surrounds children in the fields of education and social work disguises the lack of fundamental security in many of the children who are the supposed objects of care and help.

It is almost as if we cannot bear to admit and share this insecurity, so we compensate with any number of strategies and interventions, individual and collective. It is rather like putting a three-course meal in front of a child who is scared to death and therefore without appetite. I have often come across schoolchildren for whom the school curriculum and experience is completely irrelevant because of their anxiety and insecurity.[4] The way in which new 'syndromes' are introduced and described, accompanied by the prescription of specific drugs, has long made me wonder whether professionals have seriously considered the overwhelming importance of security in a child's life.

In saying this, I am seeking to do equal justice to both psychological and theological perspectives. The former has garnered much evidence about the ways in which insecurity negates the positive effects of other parts of the system, and the latter starts with the basic question of the meaning of life in the face of existential anxieties about death and nothingness.

THINKING CRITICALLY ABOUT NEEDS

One simple way of understanding the five themes is as a list of basic human needs. There are three very good examples of this approach: *Common Human Needs* by Charlotte Towle,[5] *The Needs of Children* by Mia Kellmer Pringle[6] and *The Irreducible Needs of Children* by Brazelton and Greenspan.[7] I am happy to commend them to you and have benefited from reading them. Let me summarize the irreducible needs of children as defined by Brazelton and Greenspan, so that you can see how close they are to what I seek to describe:

a) A safe, secure and nurturing environment that includes a daily relationship with at least one stable, predictable, comforting and protective adult

b) Emotional interactions geared to the child's developmental needs and level

c) Ongoing intense relationships with the same caregivers, including the primary one, early in life and throughout childhood

d) Sights, sounds, touches and other sensations tailored to the baby's unique nervous system to foster learning, language, awareness, attention and self-control
e) Experiences that build a sense of initiative and competency, including risk-taking and failure
f) Limits and expectations/structure and clear boundaries
g) Stable neighbourhoods and communities within which families can achieve these goals[8]

Despite the similarity between these 'needs' and the themes of this book, however, things are not quite that simple. First, although the five themes can be described as human needs, they are more than that. Creativity (see Chapter Seven) relates not just to need but to potential, imagination, resources and the image of God. Boundaries (see Chapter Four) are not just needed: they provide a context and shape for exploration and growth. So, although the idea of needs is a useful handle on which to hang the themes, it cannot contain the whole story.

What is more, the very notion of 'need' is not without its problems. Who is to decide what is a need and what is a longing, a wish or a desire? Who is to say when a need has been met? What is a 'good enough' meeting of need for someone to be able to function satisfactorily, psychologically and socially? Who can predict whether children will be resilient enough[9] to grow and mature without one of these fundamental human 'needs' being met? With such questions in mind, it becomes apparent that the themes cannot accurately be described as 'needs': they may be seen as desirable in the construction of a child-friendly context or world but (with the exception of security) they are not, strictly speaking, essential. For if they are not irreducible, then they are not needs.

This may sound like semantics and the splitting of hairs, but there is a lot at stake. From a faith perspective, do we, strictly speaking, ever *need* anything other than the assurance that God is with us, unfailingly, with sure and steadfast love in every situation, and that when we die we will be even more aware of his presence than we are now, while we see only 'a poor reflection as in a mirror' (1 Corinthians 13:12)? We are probably wise to pause at this stage to consider what we really mean before we continue with an exploration of the five themes.

Eric Berne, who founded Transactional Analysis, would probably prefer to describe these concepts as 'hungers'.[10] This enriches our understanding of the nature of the five themes in that it takes us into a new symbolic world, but it still does not exhaust the content or meaning of the themes. To speak of 'hungers' will inevitably tend to promote the underlying notion of a needy, wanting and underfed child. In fact, this is not actually what I take Berne to mean, but the worrying niggle is still there. Within this paradigm, where is the child who is already, in some sense, complete because he or she is created in the image of God? Where is the adult who is still hungry for love and affection?

Furthermore, both sets of categories—needs and hungers—assume that if those needs are met or hungers assuaged, some form of mature adult must be likely to result. Thus we have the stereotypes of the needy child (for whom adults provide food, shelter, education, care and so on) and the independent, functioning human adult (who has left childhood behind). These are the two coordinates that inform and map the basic construct when we talk of 'child development'. Most of what is written about children growing up—whether in education, care, psychology or children's ministry in church—assumes something of this paradigm.

We tend to have in mind some sort of identikit image of what makes a mature adult (independent, integrated, a good citizen, a parent, responsible at work and so on). Much of what societies do with and for children is driven by the attempt to create the conditions that will produce this sort of adult. These qualities of the ideal adult function as the 'learning outcomes' of a successful childhood for parents, teachers and social workers. In such meta-narratives or ideologies, the notions of ideal child and adult are a deep-seated part of the collective unconscious. They are implanted so deeply in our taken-for-granted systems and institutions that they remain mostly unquestioned and undisturbed.

In this paradigm, a baby develops physically, emotionally, psychologically, cognitively and spiritually through certain predictable stages until he or she reaches so-called maturity. Those of us who are responsible for parenting children (not to mention those who write books about it!) tend to assume that we are mature and developed, so the whole paradigm is very alluring and self-congratulatory. It is hard to acknowledge that maturity is, in some respects, a different constellation of need, and that beyond maturity there is old age or decrepitude, marked by some of the very needs that young children have but that cannot be met in the same way.

Like inappropriate extensions of the Darwinian theory of natural selection to human and even societal development, this model takes what is observable in some measure in one aspect of human life, and then applies it, whether consciously or not, to the other aspects. So it is obvious that physically, all things being equal, a baby grows. This physical growth can be measured both in terms of size and weight. There is also cognitive development, which may be less clear and predictable but is still theoretically measurable. For ease of reference, the 'normal' stages of development are usually accompanied by the ages when average or typical children are expected to reach them (I have numerous examples beside me in books and papers as I write), and before you know it, there is an assumption that emotional and even spiritual growth in some way mirrors or accompanies this physical growth.[11]

In their influential book *The Spirit of the Child*,[12] David Hay and Rebecca Nye strongly critique this way of thinking. They do not dismiss stage development theories as such, but see a problem in their narrowness: 'coming near to dissolving religions into reason and therefore childhood spirituality into nothing more than a form of immaturity or inadequacy'.

Others share their unease about this approach. One reason is that it doesn't do justice to the variety of evidence from people's life stories, another that it does not adequately reflect the many different contexts around the world. So I would like to introduce here a specifically theological contribution to thinking about the general idea of a development model. My hope is that, in time, there will be a greater integration of the theological and psycho-social perspectives. Meanwhile, I sense that, for many readers, this exposure to a theological dimension to human development will constitute a critique of their prevailing paradigm.[13]

THEOLOGICAL CONTRIBUTIONS TO THEORY

In this section, I draw largely from the insights of Karl Barth and others as reflected by James Loder in *The Logic of the Spirit*.[14] This substantial book may well provide a foundation for a much-needed conversation and interchange between theology and psycho-social theory, which those of us who are both committed Christians and also trained professionals in aspects of children's work need so badly.

Loder's challenge to traditional child and human development theory is neatly summed up in a few pages accompanied by a diagram.[15] The reader is left in no doubt that he is seeking to initiate a Copernican-type revolution in the whole way we think about human development. He is not tinkering at the edges and refining certain aspects of conventional theoretical models: like one of his mentors, Karl Barth in the field of theology, he is saying a loud 'No' to existing methods and theory and calling for a tectonic shift at the most fundamental level. He puts it like this: 'The whole configuration of human development needs to be reconceptualized.'[16] In essence, he argues that we have mistaken a circle for progress.

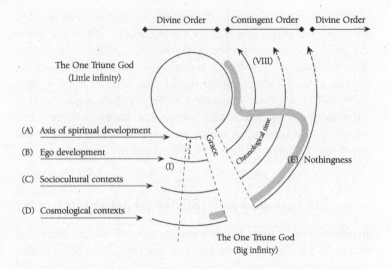

I invite you to pause and reread the last paragraph because, if we are honest, Loder's challenge comes to all of us—not least teachers and social workers—as a severe blow as well as a surprise. Are we really in the business of helping children and young people to go round in circles, to tread water, to become busy in activity that leads nowhere? Clearly there is real progress in what we observe and facilitate in children, including motor skills, language and the concept of number, so what does Loder mean? Is he really denying the validity of all of Piaget's observations on cognitive development, for example?[17] Let us see.

Loder asks us to begin by rooting our thinking theologically. This means that we attempt to see things as we believe God might see them, and we know something of his perspective as it is revealed through his word. So, for example, we know that as humans we live between two states of existence (or non-existence from the non-Christian point of view): there is existence before conception and after death. Loder calls these states 'little infinity' and 'big infinity' for ease of reference.

This big picture is marginalized in contemporary discourses but has been much more to the fore in other periods of history. When the first Christian missionaries came to Northumbria in Anglo-Saxon times, the local leaders agreed to become Christians if this new faith could help them answer the great riddle of what comes before birth and after death.[18]

Any spiritual progress or journey, from a theological perspective, is made in and through God's grace, between these two modes or grounds of existence. If we make this our starting point and framework, it begins to be possible to accept that academic degrees, motor coordination and cognitive development may not help spiritual progress one bit in any direct or observable way (although we dare not rule out the sovereignty of grace of God in any part of creation). As we ponder this challenging thought, perhaps the words of Jesus ring in our ears: 'I praise you, Father, Lord of heaven and earth, because you have hidden these things from the wise and learned, and revealed them to little children. Yes, Father, for this was your good pleasure' (Matthew 11:25–26, NIV). There is not a hint here that stages of cognitive and academic development necessarily lead people any closer to entering or comprehending the kingdom of heaven.

Then, if we take ego development as an example, it is shown in the diagram as a circle that moves neither nearer to nor further from either of the two infinities. This is not to say that it has no value—it is valuable in its own frame of reference and on its own terms—but that it does not have ultimate theological or spiritual value or significance. We might like to ponder whether a child with learning disabilities is nearer or further from the kingdom of heaven than a child prodigy. It is not an easy question to deal with appropriately, and I have come across quite different responses, from that of Frances Young[19] to that of Caroline and Mark Philps[20] and Henri Nouwen.[21] However we respond, the very question opens up the possibility that we may be on the wrong track, barking up the wrong tree. Put simply, it would be unwise, if not futile, for Christians to make cognitive development or ego development the sole basis of their theory and understanding of human spiritual development in God's sight.

Although we as Christians take time—chronological and historical—seriously (and the theory of time has shaped traditional child development theories substantially and possibly more than we have hitherto noticed), we do not make it the ultimate framework for our viewpoint.[22] If we make time our basic context for seeing and measuring human progress, we will probably tend to make sense of things by a sequence of stages of development.[23] Yet there is a dimension that we label variously spiritual, transcendent, and infinite, which cannot be captured or measured within time. There might be significant progress in ego and socio-cultural functioning, but it tells us nothing about how a human being or group relates to the intersection of time and eternity, to being and nothingness. It sidelines the basic questions of the essence and meaning of life.[24]

In circumscribing child development between the boundaries of conception and adulthood, we have not been faithful to what everyone knows—that this is to leave out most of the story. Indeed, it may not even consider the most important parts of the story. If we shift from theology and science to literature, film, art and music, we find issues and questions that go far beyond the simple model of child development into adulthood: death, origins, sin, forgiveness, atonement and so on.

Theology helps us to side with such challenges to existing paradigms by insisting that, however valuable traditional development theory may be, it is not the whole story. It will not do, if we take seriously death, nothingness, suffering and the meaning of life. For Christians, there is a perspective that starts with existential questions and departs from the ultimately meaningless circularity of indecisive existence,[25] by means of the grace and redemption that come through the life, death and resurrection of Jesus Christ.

Theology, starting from the triune God and revealed uniquely through Jesus Christ, provides a more adequate and encompassing framework for a study of human development than what is usually offered. It is not the purpose of this book to expand much more on this approach, but it is vital for the reader to realize at this stage that the book goes beyond the conventional boundaries of the study of child development and, in doing so, questions those boundaries. Future historians may well see that contemporary children's ministry in churches has swallowed the camel of traditional child development theory, contenting itself with straining out a few gnats by introducing concepts such as 'spirituality'.

One of the effects of Loder's approach is that it confirms my hesitation about introducing any age-related stages of 'child development'. It is not that these stages have no use but that we need to explore what the world of child and human development looks like without making them our ultimate frame of reference. If the Christian faith does anything in relation to time, it challenges the idea that the measurement of the clock or calendar is of ultimate significance.

We must distinguish between *kairos* and *chronos*, and be aware of the intersection of human time and eternal life.[26] This can be put another way by asking to what extent development theory pays attention to and celebrates the 'present'. It always seems to be the poor relation, sacrificed in order to reach the future goal.[27] The 'sacrament of the present moment' is not just for believers highly skilled in contemplative prayer, but may be what children celebrate routinely in their wonder and play.[28]

Models that are relevant will not only aid understandings of steady growth but will also resonate with the stormy feelings and experiences of children and families where death, birth, illness, obsessions, fears, compulsions and so much else continually erupt into life. In and through the attempt to make some sense of what is going on (the crucible of experience), there is the potential to create the conditions for deeper knowledge and growth. What is required are the faith and resilience to face the truth, in whatever shape and form it comes.

Years ago, I had an unforgettable conversation with an Austrian psychotherapist, Kurt Pick. We were sitting beside an open fire in his home in Caversham, and I imagined it must have been something like this when people talked with Paul Tournier. Kurt told me that he envied me, and I responded that I was not at all clear why that should be so. He continued by saying that although we were both what he called 'child care theoreticians', the difference between us was that he was always right! Before I had time to consider a sensitive way of querying this statement, he said, 'And you know why? Because I am retired and see no more children! Therefore, my theories are all intact and will for ever remain unchallenged. But for you, living at Mill Grove, I bet that there are many times when all your theories are in smithereens.'

He was right, and I have subsequently often been grateful to him for encouraging me to appreciate the situations and occasions when everything seems to be falling around me. When I simply do not understand what is going on, why, and what I ought to think or do, it is reassuring to see these as potentially defining moments that may become part of the continuous learning process, where daily living refines theory.[29]

One of the reasons I welcome the insights of Barth, Torrance and Loder is that my daily experience of living with children often disturbs the status quo of existing theory. So I have known the development of relationships and affection coming decades after a painful childhood, a single positive experience that is remembered as 'something we used to do', a child with learning difficulties who sees deeply into the psychology and relationships of others, family patterns that seem to recur for no reason, anger that erupts despite the most careful planning, resilience in the most hostile environments, acts of kindness where they are least expected, mental health in those deemed ill and so on. Novels are often more true to life than some textbooks.

I hope that you will try to read this book in that light. It is not trying to be dogmatic or prescriptive, but rather to describe as honestly as possible what happens when daily practice and experience are informed by and, in turn, challenge theology and psycho-social theory.

Before leaving the theological perspective, I want to say a word about how it relates to the five themes of this book. In each of the chapters that follow, I have sought to draw from biblical as well as psycho-social theory and practical experience. These biblical insights are set within an understanding of human nature and development that sees our ultimate security and significance in God's love, mercy, forgiveness and grace; his boundaries as those within which we best thrive; the new community modelled and established in and through the life, death, resurrection of Jesus Christ as the one in which we can be truly human; and his creation as the primary realm in which we little creators find greatest joy and fulfilment, when our secondary creations resonate with his.

FIVE FINGERS

As an amateur pianist I cannot get out of my mind the notion of a five-finger exercise here. The five themes can be seen as five fingers—all part of one hand and contributing to the playing of a single piece of music. We must avoid allegory, but I hope some readers will find the analogy useful. If one or more fingers are missing, it may still be possible to play the piece in recognizable form but the overall performance will be adversely affected.

What is the piece that the fingers are playing? I think we are, at heart, talking about a five-fingered exercise on a four-letter word. That word, as you know from the title of the book, is love. So I might put it like this. The fundamental need, desire, hunger, longing and potential gift of every human is to love and be loved. I want to avoid any possibility of suggesting that it is the adults (or others) who do the loving and the child who receives that love. It is a reciprocal process, perhaps best envisaged as a child discovering where and how his or her longing and potential for, and expression of, love finds requital. If love is learnt, then it is certainly not taught or received: it is a process of discovery that requires the child as the key agent in the whole process.[30]

That brings us back to very near the place where we started this chapter. If we see these five themes simply as needs or hungers, we will find it hard to know how they relate to love. Children don't simply need or hunger for love, as if it were a commodity that someone else can provide. Nor do they dispense love. Love is not like that. Love is given and received, often unconsciously and unexpectedly: it emerges through relationship, knowing, trusting, belonging, community, creativity and so on. This may help to explain why I have chosen my five themes and presented them as they are, why I have given the title to the book, and why the integration of theology and psychology is so important, for theology is willing to speak—like ordinary people, however hesitantly—of love.

STOOPING TO ENTER THE WORLD OF CHILDHOOD

So now we are ready to seek to enter or re-enter (for we were all children once) a child's world. I am assuming that my readers are adults, and that many are used to being alongside children. For this reason, I want to suggest a way of stooping to regain a sense of wonder at the size and scale of this world. I have often used this script at the beginning of teaching sessions around the world. (Another resource that I use in a similar way is the book *Children's Letters to God*.[31]) It goes like this:

Let me invite you to reconsider the relation between the adult and the child, between the adult world and the world of the child in this simple way.

I'm going to ask you now to pause, to set aside your thoughts and concerns, and to stoop very low.

Come with me as we seek to enter the child's world. It's a world we once inhabited, and yet we have been so out of touch with it, it may seem strange, even foreign to us.

We recognize the wisdom of Gibran's words as we begin to slow up, to pause, to stoop:

> *You may give them your love but not your thoughts,*
> *for they have their own thoughts.*
> *You may house their bodies but not their souls,*
> *for their souls dwell in the house of tomorrow which you*
> *cannot visit, not even in your dreams.*

But we strive to lay aside our fear of vulnerability, mental images and terminology, and as we cross the threshold we immediately have to experience what the children's writers grasp instinctively: we have entered not a classroom or an apartment. We have entered a whole new world: the child's kingdom.

To a child, a family real or imagined is a kingdom. For a significant part of childhood, the family is not just one of a number of groups and institutions: it is the world.

The family is the child's kingdom. An *ordinary kingdom* might look like this:

- Mum and Dad are king and queen.
- They make the laws of the realm.
- The sovereign territory comprises house or flat, and garden or balcony.
- The kingdom has its own unique vocabulary and traditions, its own history and myths.
- It has its yearly festivals.
- There are links with other family kingdoms through ambassadors called uncles and aunts, or gran and grandad.

- Each kingdom has a television, and patterns of life, as well as furniture, are arranged around as if it were some fixed holy shrine.
- By foreign exchange, goods enter the kingdom, many from the great neighbouring empires of Sainsbury's, Tesco, Asda and Morrisons.
- Daily conferences and summits are held with contemporaries in nurseries or schools.

But it also follows that *problems in the child's family or kingdom* will seem correspondingly huge.

The adult world may completely underestimate their scale and significance. What may seem to adults as local and temporary, for the child could well be about everywhere and affect a lifetime.

- When parents divorce, the whole kingdom is divided. It can seem like civil war, with split loyalties.
- When a family breaks up, it resembles an earthquake, with great cracks appearing in the very ground of the child's being.
- When a step-parent enters a family, it is like a change of government.
- A burglary can resemble an invasion by a hostile power, leaving scars that remain long after the insurance has covered replacement goods.
- Physical injuries can haunt the memory like war wounds.
- A house move can seem like an evacuation or emigration, with the loss of familiar landmarks and territory. (Can you imagine Pooh and friends taken out of the familiar Hundred-Acre Wood?)
- A broken promise or lie is an abrogation of a fundamental treaty or covenant.
- Abuse is totalitarian aggression and savage oppression.
- Poverty can mean famine.
- A visit to the DSS can seem like a delegation approaching IMF.

You can do the rest for yourselves if you stoop low enough to enter the child's kingdom.

Adult timescales, logic and distinctions have as much place in this world as a sceptical theologian in Narnia.

Adults are as bad at understanding the 'feel-good' factor in families as chancellors are in national economies.

The silent, inner cries of children, masked by smiles or busyness, can go unheard.

Children are princes and princesses of these kingdoms. No wonder *The Little Prince*, *The Lord of the Flies*, *Snow White* and *Cinderella* strike such chords!

Children see themselves at the heart of their kingdom. They assume that their actions, or even their thoughts, cause much of what happens. 'No fault' divorce may be, to them, their fault. Their overwhelming sense of guilt and responsibility can seem out of proportion to adults who don't understand.

Later, they discover their kingdom to be but one little component of what adults call the nation or state.

As you read what follows, I invite you never to forget the disparity between the two worlds. Security, boundaries, significance, community and creativity may mean so much more to a child than we can grasp. The stakes are so very high. I would not go so far as to suggest that you and I are about to stand on holy ground, but we are entering a very special world and we will need to tread with great respect.

✣

Chapter Three

SECURITY

Enough for me to keep my soul tranquil and quiet like a child in its mother's arms.

Psalm 131:2 (JB)

BEING HELD

We begin the description and exploration of the five themes with security.[1] Security has to do with the most basic belief that there is always somewhere to shelter and hide in the fiercest storm; a rock that will not move when everything else seems to give way; a centre that will hold when things feel as if they are falling apart.

Perhaps the best metaphor for this is the experience of 'being held'. The newborn and growing baby experiences being literally held in the mother's or father's arms, and this is where our life outside the womb usually starts—held at our mother's breast. We were 'held', that is, kept safe and nurtured, in our mother's womb, and now it is being held that takes some of the place of this fundamental longing and need.

Throughout history and now, at the moment that you are reading these words, there are thousands upon thousands of little children who lack this most fundamental of experiences. War, famine and disease, individually or collectively, undermine, remove and demolish anything that might normally provide this security, this holding. The death or loss of parents (for example, through hospitalization, imprisonment or migration) is one of the ways in which major problems make their presence felt in the life of the young child.

Being held is not just about the food, shelter and protection that contribute to a sense of well-being. It is the basis of the bonding and attachment that are vital to the development of self-esteem, identity and the growth of love. It is more than the protection of a child from external factors that cause fear and harm. It is essential in the face of internal anxieties, feelings and fears. One of these anxieties is the anger that wells up and threatens to overwhelm the child. It is sometimes described as 'temper', but its roots are deep within the psyche and it is not so much about relations with others and matters of self-control (though it may develop into these issues) as about a raging battle within the child between feelings and forces of life and death. When this conflict erupts into uncontrollable crying and obvious deep distress, it is vital that the child is held—probably literally in the arms of a sensitive and loving parent. In this way, and unconsciously, the child is reassured that even the deepest fears and feelings are 'OK' in the sense that they will not lead to his or her destruction.

At the end of Chapter Two we reminded ourselves just how high the stakes are for children: there are times when, for them, it is not just a part of the world that is under pressure, but everything, everywhere. There is nowhere that is safe. It is striking how often children who have come to Mill Grove as a result of bereavement, loss, neglect, stress and so on describe what they experienced as an earthquake or tsunami. They often use the word 'shattered'.[2] Their whole world has disintegrated. There has been a cracking of the ground of their being. The tectonic plates of their lives have come apart. They seem to suggest that they are in danger of, if not actually experiencing, falling into an abyss—an infinite void that has opened up in their lives.

This echoes experiences more common than we might suppose. The children I am talking about have experienced very tangible and concrete threats and aggression, but the phantoms and fears of all children are of this magnitude. In their inner worlds, there are feelings and flights of fancy that are beyond control and dwarf the child and his or her protective mechanisms into insignificance. You may recall some of these fears from your own childhood. The fear of the dark is a common one. You may have overcome it, but don't let this detract from the desperate nature of the feelings that it engendered. This is not the place to discuss children's literature, but ghosts, dragons and monsters lurk everywhere—and Grimm's fairy stories are to do with the same territory of experience.

Recently, I was walking with friends in North Wales and, as the winter sun was setting over the Lleyn Peninsular, I asked one of them how his children were coping with the separation and divorce of their parents. He said that in the past six months they were doing much better than before. When I asked him why he thought this was so, he reflected in his own words that 'they felt much more secure'. Because I was in the middle of writing this chapter at the time, my ears pricked up and I dared to probe further, wondering what the constituent elements of this feeling of security might be. He said that it was about predictability, reliability. They 'knew where they were' at last.

It turned out that the favourite game of one of these children was a particular version of 'Hide and seek', in which he ran away and was then found and held in his parent's arms, pretending to get away. He asked to play the same game again and again. There is little doubt that, in this way, he was unconsciously re-enacting his own real experiences and fears and gaining reassurance every time he was found and held.

As it happened, it was on a journey to the same place in North Wales that I called to mind two of the times when I had felt most vulnerable and anxious, and how, on reflection, I had found comfort. One was the tragic death of my wife's parents and one of her brothers in a car accident on the way to our house. In the following months there were, no doubt, many ways in which our family was 'held' (including routines, our faith, and the support and prayers of family and friends), but there was one song that I played and sang to more than any other at the time. It was by Adrian Snell—a setting of

Psalm 27 called 'Wherever I go, you are there'. A line in the middle of the song goes, 'Hold me like a child within your arms.' I have no doubt that this prayer and this unconscious association brought unique comfort to me over a period of months during which it felt as if the ground had opened up under our feet.

The second anxious time was when one of my immediate family was desperately needing me. To be there, I had to make a complicated car journey of several hundred miles, largely through the night. I arrived just before eight o'clock in the morning, tired and anxious to the point of feeling overwhelmed. The situation seemed crushingly bleak.

As I came to a halt, I realized I was beside a cathedral and that the service of Holy Communion was just about to start. On the spur of the moment, I joined the group of believers in a side chapel, grateful for the space that the 1662 Prayer Book service allowed for personal prayer and reflection, and the predictability of the whole service.[3] No one spoke to me; apart from receiving the bread and wine and a handshake, there was no human contact. For this I was profoundly grateful because I treasured the security of the anonymity of the experience.

On reflection, what proved to be the most reassuring aspect of the service was the presence of the huge stone walls of this ancient cathedral. I sat beside one of them: they were more than ten feet thick and had been in place for hundreds of years. It was in and through them that I felt safe. As I think back to the service, I cannot recall the readings for the day and I cannot say whether I listened to or heard them, but the walls remain vividly etched in my memory. They 'held' me.

I have described in *Celebrating Children* a little of the life of one child who came to Mill Grove, who, as far as anyone could ascertain, had never experienced 'being held' by his mother, family or schools. As a result, his life became a sequence of exclusions from family, foster care and schools because no one could contain his rage. People were fearful of his feelings—and this was perhaps nothing beside the fear that he experienced himself. He received a consistent message that his feelings always led to the collapse of his whole world and led to another move. Things were always falling apart.

It was just possible—though we were stretched to the limits—for Mill Grove to provide a holding environment for him. The key element was that we refused to exclude or reject him. I have little doubt that this experience of 'holding' was just in time. A few months later and no one could have done it. He would have been at risk of being placed in some form of clinical or custodial care, where the holding is done by locks and bars of one form or another. For both of us, a highly symbolic moment came when we were bouldering together in North Wales. We reached a point where I could go no further. He took over the lead and, from the top, he leaned down and took hold of my hand. He knew that I trusted him and was now relying on him to hold me.

'Holding', as I have said, is at the heart of the formation of bonds of attachment, and it is important to be aware that although, for little children, we are talking about literal holding, we are using the term primarily as a metaphor. One of the best descriptions of 'holding' that I know is by the psychotherapist Dan Hughes. In his book *Building the Bonds of Attachment*,[4] he deals with how to provide a holding experience when a child has formed no satisfactory attachments. This, of course, resonates with my experience at Mill Grove. The response needs deep understanding, teamwork, supervision and faith.

There are many ways in which to experience the assurance that rage is not the final and devastating word in the life of a child. What the child needs is 'firm arms' around him or her, conveying the sense that this rage will not get completely out of control, will not overwhelm; it will not provoke equal and opposite reactions that will in turn overwhelm; it will not provoke a letting go of the child that leaves him or her feeling no possibility of respite from these primal screams. In our contemporary culture, which is so concerned about protecting children from inappropriate touching, we may well find that we are on occasions inadvertently depriving children of the security that they need. It is a very difficult balance, but security in this sense is so important that it must at the very least be considered as part of the equation.

In theological terms (as well as in the psychotherapeutic literature), we are dealing here with the very ground of our being; with the 'little infinity', death, nothingness, the fear of non-being and destruction. Often, policies and practices of governments and NGOs seeking to help children in need, or 'at risk', focus their activity largely on the meeting of physical needs. Responses concentrate on the provision of shelter, food, clothing, the basics of survival and physical protection from those people, institutions and forces that threaten the safety and well-being of the child.

Heaven knows there is more than enough of this physical oppression, which puts survival at risk, but we need to acknowledge that within the soul and being of every child there is the fear of annihilation. War and famine will prompt, exacerbate and escalate this fear, but the absence of such external factors will not remove it.[5] This is confirmed by the way in which children in rich and poor countries alike show evidence of just such a fear. Wealth is no protection against it. It is possible that we are witnessing more mental health problems among children and young people in the Western world now than at any time in history. There are some things that parents (and substitute parents) can do to protect children from harm, but we need to recognize that the fears and anxieties go even deeper.

The word 'security' seeks to encompass all of this. It is about internal and external factors and forces—the personal, the familial, the communal, the national and the international. No one can erect physical defences to ensure that a child knows genuine security. The way to a sense of security is through relationships and experiences which lead the child, over time, to trust that somehow and somewhere security is to be found, and to internalize this trust.

ATTACHMENT

Attachment theory is perhaps the key to understanding security. The clinician John Bowlby, whom I have already mentioned, has thrown new light on the ways in which humans develop, through this theory. In view of Bowlby's extensive output, I have limited my references here to one of his works, which is actually a collection of reflective lectures with the title *A Secure Base: Clinical Applications of Attachment Theory*.[6]

Attachment instincts and associated behaviours have been observed in many parts of the spectrum of animal and human species, notably between mothers (and, in some cases, fathers) and their infants. They are also common throughout human life, adult as well as infant. Bowlby sees them as universal and the norm in human behaviour. They have biological roots related to the provision of food, shelter and comfort. The vulnerable child has a reflex reaction to turn to a parent figure for what we are calling security. Although it has biological roots, however, Bowlby is clear that it is not just about physical survival. He writes of the very strong and intense emotions that accompany such behaviour, and my own experience alongside hurting and anxious children confirms his observations.

In a number of ways, the parent conveys to the child sensitivity to his or her needs and feelings. Bowlby describes some of these ways, and comments, 'If it goes well, there is joy and a sense of security. If it is threatened, there is jealousy, anxiety and anger. If it is broken, there is grief and depression.'[7] This attachment behaviour and sensitivity begins in the mother's womb.

The central feature of this whole approach to parenting (which includes the notion that it takes a village to parent) is the provision of a secure base. Let me allow Bowlby to describe what he means:

The provision by both parents of a secure base from which a child or an adolescent can make sorties into the outside world and to which he can

return knowing for sure that he will be welcomed when he gets there,
nourished physically and emotionally, comforted if distressed, reassured if
frightened. In essence this role is one of being available, ready to respond
when called upon to encourage and perhaps assist, but to intervene
actively only when clearly necessary.[8]

You can use whatever images are most helpful to envisage this
secure base. Perhaps the picture of a harbour or port is one of the
best. A harbour is a place of safety and shelter from storms, and
represents the known world—what we might think of as home or
homeland—but it is not a place you aim for in the anticipation of
staying there. It is a place to which you can retreat but where you
can then prepare for the next voyage. Without a harbour, a ship will
ultimately run out of provisions and will falter, if not sink.

So it is emotionally with human beings—especially, but not
exclusively, little children. At first they need to be in or very near this
'harbour', and they rarely venture out of its sight without feelings of
anxiety, dread and fear. As they get older, though, if the attachment
behaviour is predictable and sensitive, they become more confident
that their base is secure.

Throughout these early years, there is the serious risk that
should the parents fall ill, be missing or die, the whole project will
falter, with neither the harbour to shelter in nor any desire to
explore the rest of the world. The harbour is necessary as a base for
exploration and, for humans, exploration is the essence of growth
and development. In a 'good enough' secure base,[9] the parents do
not desire to make the child dependent on them in such a way that
the child prefers the harbour to the sea, with its wide oceans,
predictable tides and capricious weather. The parents will rather
encourage the autonomy of the child while always remaining in
touch and available.

Part of this whole dynamic, which we will explore more fully in
the next chapter, is about providing the right kind and amount of
'space'. If it is restrictive, the child 'can't breathe' and initiative and

self-esteem will be stifled; if it is too loose, then the child's anxiety is not assuaged enough to allow confident exploration. Rowan Williams has looked at this issue in his perceptive book, *Lost Icons*,[10] where he discusses how, in children's books by Enid Blyton, the child characters have adventures in which they usually have to rely on their ingenuity and bravery to see them through, but in which they always have an adult close enough to return to for comfort, safety and advice, if things get completely out of hand.

This is where Bowlby and others who take this line face a problem with common human assumptions and language. As we noted in the previous chapter, the prevailing paradigm tends to see the little child as vulnerable, dependent and in need of protection and care, while at the other end of the spectrum is the mature, independent and capable adult. Therefore, it is usually assumed that human beings grow out of the need for a secure base.

In fact, while children manifest an open and obviously practical and physical tendency to retreat to their base, behaviour in adults shows that at times of stress and anxiety there always remains the tendency to seek out and replicate attachment behaviour. This can, of course, be a case of infantile and destructive regression to dependence, but returning to a secure base is sensible for anyone who knows it is time to seek the succour and safety of home, when the storms are too fierce or prolonged to survive without help.[11]

When considering children and the growth of love, one of the primary tasks is to understand and nurture this process of appropriate attachment between parents and children. It helps greatly if we realize that we (that is, 'villagers' other than the actual parents of the child) have a part to play in creating and maintaining the harbour. For example, schools may overlook attachment behaviour in planning the deployment of teachers year by year, or they might consider adopting Rudolph Steiner's approach and try to keep the children with the same teacher for the duration of the pupil's school career. For some pupils (and not only boarders), school may be a vital part of the attachment process. The same is true of neighbourhoods and faith-based communities. Clubs and social groups also have their part to play.

Another related task is to do all we can to prevent anything that would undermine this attachment, whether at the personal or the macro level. (This is one of the subjects of Chapter Nine.)

SECURITY UNDER THREAT

What happens if the child's secure base is overwhelmed or destroyed? What interventions do we make and based on what principles? I have already made it clear that I am not an advocate of one approach or method rather than another, but I have come to see that our primary task is to do something about recreating this secure base. I can put this another way: we may have lots of good ideas and programmes, including counselling, therapy, foster care, support and the like, but if the child feels threatened to the point of being insecure, all this effort is likely to have little effect. The child can vest little or no effort in anything in life while there is an underlying insecurity.

I recall Bowlby making exactly this point in a seminar in Edinburgh in 1970: the primary instinct of the child is survival, and the lack of a secure base means that survival is at stake. At such times there is no energy or desire for food, sex or exploration. All that matters is safety and survival. You can see this in cases of eating disorders, for example.[12]

Therefore, it is my strong belief that caring and resourceful adults must make it their primary task to address this most basic of all human needs. I am not saying that we must always seek to be the sole or main providers of that secure base for every child—that is as impossible as it is undesirable—but we should make it a primary task to identify where, how and by whom the secure base can be reconstructed. Sadly, a more common response is to hide the issue in our busyness.

It is encouraging to see that children are often active participants in this process: they are essential and resourceful partners in the creation of a secure base. Such a base is a many-textured thing. Changing the analogy for a moment from harbour to bird's nest, some birds draw material for their nests from a wide range of sources—and so it is with secure bases for humans. Before any intervention, we need to discover what has gone into making up the child's present or previous secure base, which may include parents, family home, extended family, community, garden, trees, toys, belongings, patterns of life, school, church, games, songs and so on. These things are not all always concrete providers of the attachment base, but often function symbolically.

My experience from different parts of the world has taught me that children find an alternative secure base in many and varied ways. Usually, parents or parent figures will have fostered good enough attachment behaviours, but then all sorts of other people, places and things become part of the lifelong process—maybe a hobby, an object or a team. We must tread carefully lest we unwittingly destroy the very thing we are seeking to create. Emma Adam has written about the importance of environmental stability in the life of a child. So much attention has been focused on the separation of parents and emotional relationships that the link between child and physical place has tended to be overlooked.[13]

D.W. Winnicott's 'transitional objects' are an important element in this process.[14] He calls the space between people in which relationships occur (the 'inner' and 'outer' world) 'transitional space'. In this liminal space, transitional objects are of importance both physically and symbolically. For the very young child, who is beginning to understand the difference between 'me' and 'not me', objects (like Linus' blanket, or a teddy bear, a sound or word, a tree, or a step on the stairs) allow the fantasy of the child about his or her wishes towards the mother to be represented. They are vital in the process of internalizing the presence of the mother, and thus the mother–child relationship, when she is absent.

A salutary example that constantly alerts me to the agency and choices of children involves a rowan tree in North Wales. On the eastern edge of the mountain range dominated by Cadair Idris, not far south of Snowdon, and near the place where Mary Jones set off in search of her famous Bible in Bala, there is a long escarpment of inhospitable rock and ledges stretching for perhaps two miles. There are very few bushes and trees here: it is not a place where you would ever think of planting them. Lichens and moss thrive in the damp and windy conditions. Twenty years or more ago, however, I noticed a rowan tree (mountain ash is another name), growing in splendid but apparently doomed isolation. I expected it to fall or be blown over but, as the years have passed, I have watched it grow. It is now firmly and securely rooted and will no doubt see out its allotted span of years on its unlikely perch.

Had this tree been a child, I guess we might have thought of it as an orphan: we would certainly have considered it lonely and its situation precarious and, if we had done what is at present called a 'risk assessment', I think we would have moved it. Such an intervention, we know, might well cause it lasting if not irreparable damage, but my guess is that we would have done so all the same, in order to place it in conditions that we deemed to be more conducive to its survival and growth.

I wonder how many children have been the objects of well-meaning adult interventions that have failed to recognize the security and potential of the unlikely contexts in which those children were living. We have taken action to move them from a familiar to an unfamiliar context, at great risk to their sense of security. Perhaps there is more security 'on the streets' for some children, which we fail to recognize because we are locked into conventional patterns of how security is experienced.

I may have made this link because of my life at Mill Grove. Here, although we live as a family, we are officially categorized as a 'children's home' (as distinct from a family, adoptive home or foster care) providing 'residential child care'. Social workers do all they can to keep children out of such places, seeing them as a last resort. If a child is unfortunate enough, in their eyes, to have arrived in such a place, they try to move the child on as quickly as possible. Yet, for years, research that has paused to consider the views and reflections of the children themselves has found that a significant proportion say they prefer to live in such places: these young people have found something of security in them. This always 'surprises' the professional establishment and the media, largely because they do not take the children and their views seriously enough to change their own paradigms and perspectives.[15]

My own view is that such a change would take a fundamental reassessment of the whole fabric of our society, which is, of course, unlikely in the extreme, so we continue to move children to the places of our choosing despite what the rowan tree represents and proves. I find this rowan tree very comforting because the conditions in which it thrives are really hostile. It reminds me that children have resilience, and we do well to make this quality a non-negotiable part of our policies and planning.

In addition to thinking about whether or not to move a particular child whom we perceive to be at risk, we also need to think of all that undermines security in children in our 'taken for granted' world. There are the obvious factors such as the deterioration of the relationship between a child's parents, separation, divorce and loss. But there are less obvious ones, such as the short-termism of much family intervention, career moves that mean a child does not see the same social worker over a period of time, and an educational system that does not rate security as high priority. There is the possibility that the globalization of the media will provide much worrying, ill-digested information that eats into a child's security. Take 9/11, for example: I heard about it from one of my daughters who had been watching television when the events unfolded. Neither my wife nor I was present, and for a period of perhaps an hour she sat traumatized by the pictures and news reports. How do we calculate the effect on her and millions like her?

SECURITY IN THE BIBLE

The Bible is full of examples of everything that threatens security. Read as a whole, it is anything but a neat, anodyne, sentimentalized children's story. I recall once, when I was running a bookshop, a mother dropped by in search of an Easter book for her child. I showed her some, but she was anxious about the effect that pictures of Jesus on the cross might have on her girl. It became clear to me that she was not looking for a biblical version of Easter so much as a Warner/Disney chocolate box cover with Easter bunnies and the like—something full of life and warmth with no trace of the agonies (and ecstasies) of the real story.

This is not the place to attempt an overall summary of the Bible, but I will give examples of what I mean. The Bible starts with creation, and the story has hints of darkness, chaos and nothingness, right from the first verses. When we get to the book of Revelation, there is a cosmic battle going on between these forces of darkness and God's light and life. If security is to be found in all this, it is not the sort of security that comes from taking Valium and separating ourselves from real-life struggles against the odds.

In the Bible we find monsters of the ocean and the land— Leviathan and Behemoth; we find wars, famines, murder, incest, rape, deceit, slavery, plagues, earthquakes, civil wars, revolutions or invasions overshadowing every event. The birth of Jesus, like the birth of Moses, takes place in the context of the systematic murdering of baby boys. This 'insecurity' (that which threatens security) occurs at every level, from the intrapersonal experience of individual human beings through to families, tribes and nations. The universe itself is shown to be set in a context of death and extinction.

We find individuals such as Job and Jeremiah, wrestling with how to continue living with integrity and peace: their struggles are described in what some might consider inordinate detail. Esther and her people are threatened with extinction through ethnic cleansing; Jesus struggles in Gethsemane in a way that recalls his 40 days fasting and being tested. This period recalls the 40 years of the Israelites in the wilderness—a timescale which is as nothing compared to the 430 years that the Hebrews spent in slavery, calling out apparently in vain to their God.

One of the things that so-called 'children's Bibles' do is to filter out most of these shadowy, threatening, ugly, evil, dark elements of the narrative—and this is very significant for us all, because many Christian adults still depend heavily on what they learnt at Sunday school as a basis for their understanding of the Bible. Perhaps the best analysis of this process and its effects is by Gretchen Wolff Pritchard, in *Offering the Gospel to Children*. She suggests that children are being offered a 'distorted canon', and summarizes her thesis thus:

The greatest problem with these children's Bibles is their distortion of the Old Testament canon, and the implications of this for children's ability to understand the Bible not as 'a story', but as 'my story'. For the heart of the Scriptures is a continuing pattern of exile and return, of loss, hope and restoration, of new life out of renunciation and death. And it emerges not only from narrative, but from prophecy, psalm, and hymns; from vision and exhortation; from parables, image and metaphor.

This pattern recurs in the Hebrew Bible in three great movements. The first is the primeval exile from the Garden of Eden, echoed in the call to Abraham to leave his kindred and his country and seek a land of promise. The second is the bondage in Egypt of the children of Israel, their deliverance in the Exodus, their entry into the land, and the building of Jerusalem, the joy of the whole earth. The third is the faithlessness of the people, the destruction of Jerusalem, the Babylonian Captivity, and the promise, beyond hope, that the dry bones will live.[16]

One of the main reasons I have been working on a new edition of the Bible for 20 years is so that children and families around the world can read the *whole* Bible for themselves. It is my experience of living at Mill Grove that has made such a major commitment of time and energy necessary. 'Children's Bibles', like many traditional Sunday school lessons, tend to stay with what is comforting and neat. So, for example, they never include the end of the story of David and Goliath, when David walks around holding the giant's severed head (1 Samuel 17:54), or when Saul puzzlingly asks who David is (vv. 55–58).

I have seen the need for a complete text that includes the difficult bits, so that the real lives of children and families, with all their messiness and unsatisfactory 'conclusions' and events, find resonance in the stories of the Bible. The two stories (the narrative of the scriptures and the biography of the reader) are then allowed to work on each other dialectically.

I have also been working for a similar period on a book called *In the Meantime*, which meditates on 40 periods in the Bible when nothing seems to be happening—or when everything seems to be going wrong. Over and over again, when I have expounded some of these periods in sermons, people have spoken to me afterwards of how comforting it is to know that there is a precedent for the unresolved conflicts and problems in their own lives and the life of the church fellowship.

The Bible is anything but a cosy collection of reassuring stories. Why, then, is it so comforting to so many people? We might venture to ask, how and where do the readers find security in it? Despite the many threats to security that we have noted in the Bible, security is rock-like through both Old and New Testaments.

One way of seeing the Bible is as a story of 'salvation'. It has been called the narrative of God's saving acts. Where rescue, healing, forgiveness and liberation are called for, the Bible tells how God (in his own way and time) hears, comes alongside his people and provides security for them in the midst of the gravest of dangers. There are many descriptions of how God does this, culminating in the life, death and resurrection of Jesus Christ. Jesus' death, with the shedding of his blood, is the event that draws together every other act of God. It has been described as a ransom, a sacrifice, redemption, salvation, liberation, a substitution, atonement and adoption. There are many symbols and metaphors of its meaning and the way it works, but in the final analysis they all add up to one underlying truth: the blood of Jesus provides a safe place (safe space) for the individual believer and for the household or community of faith.

When Jesus told his anxious disciples that he was going to leave them, he promised that the reason was 'to prepare a place for each of you' (John 14:2). That is what his death means for his followers. The 'place' he speaks of is not to be taken primarily as a literal physical enclosure, such as a room or mansion—it is the experience through Jesus Christ of security, safety and well-being—and it is not to be found by running away from difficulties, by infantile regression or by sentimentality. Rather, it is to be found by taking up our cross, daily. It is discovered by working through pain and suffering, not running away from them.

In the early part of the Jewish scriptures, security is often found in actual physical structures and realities—for example, Noah's ark, a promised land, and Jerusalem, the walled city set on a hill. After the fall of Jerusalem in 586BC, however, there comes the extraordinary literature of the great prophets, including late Isaiah, Jeremiah, Ezekiel and the so-called 'minor prophets'. Without Jerusalem, its temple and the yearly festivals and worship, we might expect that the security of the chosen people will be undermined, but the opposite turns out to be the case. A new sense of God's presence and providence is in evidence. The experience of God has become internalized so that there is no need for reliance on physical evidence of his saving presence and character. (It is worth noting that the exile and its associated prophetic literature helped to provide the basis for the extraordinary resilience of the Jewish people in the face of great testings, including the Holocaust, to this very day.)

This mirrors the development in a child: the physical presence of the mother and her breast, which are necessary for security and well-being at first, eventually become internalized so that the child is able to be away from her for longer and longer periods and get into deeper and deeper adventures without anxiety becoming overwhelming.

The Psalms are one of the most precious treasure hoards of biblical symbols that explore the security to be found when material security is absent—when the mountains tremble, when fire engulfs, when the flood overwhelms and when there is no human being or agency to help.[17] One of the most simple and beautiful is Psalm 131, quoted at the head of this chapter: 'But I have learnt to feel safe and satisfied, just like a young child on its mother's lap. People of Israel, you must trust the Lord now and for ever' (vv. 2–3, CEV). One of the most memorable, of course, is Psalm 23: 'I may walk through valleys as dark as death, but I won't be afraid. You are with me' (v. 4). There are abundant images of 'being held' throughout the Psalms, including arms, shelter, rock, shade, high towers, strong towers, walls and armies.

Elsewhere in the Bible, similar assurances of security can be found. Towards the very end of his final speech to the people of Israel, as he prepares to bid them farewell, Moses says, 'The eternal God is our hiding place; he carries us in his arms. When God tells you to destroy your enemies, he will make them run. Israel, you will live in safety; your enemies will be gone. The dew will fall from the sky, and you will have plenty of grain and wine. The Lord has rescued you and given you more blessings than any other nation. He protects you like a shield and is your majestic sword' (Deuteronomy 33:27–29).

In addition, we find the idea of God as the Shepherd of his people. This is one of the all-pervading images of the Bible, and Jesus takes it upon himself in a memorably reassuring way: 'My sheep know my voice, and I know them. They follow me, and I give them eternal life, so that they will never be lost. No one can snatch them out of my hand' (John 10:27–28).

SECURITY IN WORSHIP

Worship that is authentically Christian will always be permeated by such images and truths and, at the same time, be fully alert to the forces and realities that threaten security. Thus, children who are fully part of the worshipping community will find themselves constantly in touch with the fragility and messiness of life and the forces of evil and darkness, while at the same time being reassured by God's faithfulness, mercy and grace. The very nature of the worship is testimony to the fact that security triumphs over insecurity, light over darkness, safety over fear, and life over death. Life in such a community of faith is living testimony to the fundamental and ultimate security that is not dependent upon feelings. Nothing in heaven, upon earth, or under the earth can separate me from the love of God (see Romans 8:38–39). Is there a deeper source or sense of security to be found?

The shaking of the foundations of the Jewish people has been profoundly disturbing, but their trust in God, reflected in and strengthened by continuing acts of worship, has withstood all that has been hurled against them—and this is the ground in which Christian worship has taken root. It celebrates the story that against all the odds, Jesus Christ, having been crucified as a criminal, was raised to life, and that through him God is reconciling the world to himself. Faith, a vital element of security, is the 'evidence of things not seen' (Hebrews 11:1, AV), and those who believe in Jesus without having seen him are greatly blessed (John 20:29). In this way, security is open to all who believe irrespective of the evidence of their eyes and their situations. It is possible to face anything and anyone, not with delusions of grandeur but with a quiet confidence, as part of a believing community, that God is thoroughly to be relied upon: 'I can do everything through him who gives me strength' (Philippians 4:13, NIV).

The internalization of this belief and hope is recorded in the words of thousands of Christian hymns and songs, and it is through these that children most often find the heart of the story, the heart of God—through these songs, through the Bible stories of the history of God's people and through the parables of Jesus. Because ultimate security does not depend on fortresses, physical power and speed, we should never underestimate the power of these stories and the worship in which they are communicated and re-enacted. The place of the Christian community is rarely to entertain children or to keep them interested and amused: the task is far more important than that. It is to provide the basis, the foundations, for the development of a sense of well-being and security, rooted deeply in the nature and character of God, the history of his people and his saving acts.

Therefore, it is one of the most important of tasks for Christian families and the church, at times of worship, to tell and retell and celebrate these stories in their ruggedness and context. At the same time, through fellowship and prayer, it is vital to create the context in which children can bring their real concerns, suffering and fears into the open and connect them to the revelation of God's story.

The reality of world history is that human beings and communities have known actual catastrophes that have threatened their very existence. Whether or not we believe in Jung's theory of the collective unconscious, it is not hard to imagine that this history finds its way into the memories of individuals and communities. There is understandable fear and anxiety that threaten the sense of well-being in people. It is not realistic to promise anyone that they are beyond the reach of such catastrophes but, if there is a source of hope that can transcend them, this is of all things the most valuable.

RECOGNIZING SECURITY

How do we know that this security has been established in a child? One of the simplest measures in a community is whether there is evidence of humour. Yes, I really mean this. Where there is security, humour will flourish, and often in the darkest and most trying of times. Another measure is the readiness of a child to take risks and to explore. Without security there will be little scope for genuine experimentation, creative imagination and play—and, of course, part of this process is trust.

What is the opposite? How do we know when security has not been established? It has to do with defensiveness, which will show itself in either attack or withdrawal. The possibility of conversation and self-criticism is limited in an insecure person: everything tends to be construed as a threat to that person's well-being.

As I visit different places of worship week by week, I sometimes find a situation in which prayer and worship is defensive, parroted and repetitive. Again and again the truths of the Christian story are told, recited and prayed, but, instead of being deeply internalized and 'taken for granted', they seem more like a retreat from real life. It is as if the people in these communities would like to stay there for ever rather than using them as a base for exploration.

I like the phrase 'taken for granted' in this context: a child who is secure will take for granted the parents' continuing love and concern, even when the parent is absent. So it is with the adult Christian. A secure faith does not have to be stated and restated, for it is already experienced. Those who are always concerned about 'assurance' probably lack security, and those who are determined to share the good news with others at every possible opportunity may be covering up a fundamental insecurity. On the other hand, those who are secure can live out the good news without the overriding imperative constantly to remind themselves and others of it. This security may therefore tend to be unstated—even invisible at times—but, to those who read more deeply, it is in constant evidence through actions, empathy and conversation.

I recall a child who was so insecure that in any group, however small or familiar, he was constantly calling out, 'I'm here.' His experience of life was so insecure that even when there were adults present, he was fearful that they might not be noticing him. Unless they gave him all their attention, he was insecure. Perhaps many prayers are like that: 'God, do you realize that I am perishing? Have you forgotten me? Do you care about me any more?' The antithesis of this is the relationship between Jesus and his Father as portrayed in John's Gospel: Jesus is completely secure in his Father's good pleasure. He does not need to boast about it, to parade it. It shines through every conversation and interaction. The Christian's security, too, is to be found in and through Jesus' secure relationship with his Father.

CODA

When Dr Barnardo first encountered Jim Jarvis in the East End of London—homeless, destitute and without an advocate—he asked him whether he had ever heard of Jesus. Jim apparently thought that Jesus was the Pope, so Barnardo told Jim the old, old story of Jesus and his love.[18] For several years, Dr Gundelina Velazco, a psychologist from the Philippines, has been introducing street children to the stories and person of Jesus. Given the importance of security, and all that Jesus Christ is and offers, we would do well to consider how many and to what degree Christian agencies have been so engaged in practical action to help such children that they have overlooked one of their most precious and enduring resources.

·⊹·

Chapter Four

BOUNDARIES

'You may eat fruit from any tree in the garden, except the one that has the power to let you know the difference between right and wrong.'

Genesis 2:16–17

HOLDING TAKES NEW SHAPES AND FORMS

As we move our focus from the theme of security to boundaries (meaning norms, acceptable behaviour, rules and the like), it immediately becomes apparent that the two overlap and are interconnected. In some ways, they have similar elements, and that is how it is with each of the five themes of this book. They are not discrete entities like the pieces of a jigsaw so much as connecting threads and patterns in a tapestry. Another way of seeing them is as different perspectives on, or lenses through which we perceive, core experiences and realities, and it is not always clear which precedes which.

If the reader sees boundaries as being essential to a child's experience of security, I agree. The arms within which a baby is held could be described as the most basic and fundamental of boundaries —perhaps the archetypal boundary that all other boundaries mirror, from which they derive and, in time, develop, expand and multiply. We cannot exist without boundaries, whether as notional individuals or as social groups, but neither can we remain within our mothers' arms. We must be, and usually wish to be (in the words of the hymn 'Now thank we all our God'), 'blessed on our way'.

As we consider boundaries, we will see that we are also moving on from the existential fear of being overwhelmed, lost and dying. The child who knows a secure base is ready for exploration, but the process of exploration must have boundaries if it is not to threaten the very base that made it possible. Because, in John Donne's words, 'no man is an island', the growing child has to be helped to understand the basic categories of human and social life. What belongs to her? What belongs to his parents? What is shared?

What does the concept of boundaries include? Some have suggested discipline; regulation and rules as alternatives: my intention is to include but go beyond these suggestions. I hope to cover predictability, patterns of life and routines. There is an underlying sense of structure, reliability and the knowledge of something solid and firm inherent in the nature of what we mean by boundaries. They are not a wish list for an ideal world, but the grounds of practical living and experience.[1]

WITHOUT BOUNDARIES

As you know, I have spent most of my life alongside children and young people who have lacked basic security and secure attachments. So what has their experience of life been like? It is a mass of contradictory feelings and events welded together in the conscious and unconscious mind like metamorphic rock. Such children commonly lack the sense of a place where they started from, a place that can be, for them, home or homeland. This lack is often disguised by the formation of an imaginary world (rather like that of Piglet and Eeyore), which is completely ideal and to which they sometimes retreat in their imaginations—like a rudimentary garden of Eden. Whereas a genuine experience of attachment and bonding gives a child a strong sense of a starting point and a base for exploration, children who lack this experience do not have the very first element essential for any safe exploration. Consequently, their mental maps and their physical knowledge of the geographical world are poor, and I have noticed that mathematics is often a weak area for them. Mathematical understanding needs a firm starting point—something 'given'.

The 'world' or 'kingdom' of these children (see Chapter Two) is clearly verging on chaos—civil war—with the rumble of feared earthquakes and volcanoes in the consciousness. They have tried, with all the creativity and ingenuity of little children, to make sense of what has been happening to them, but it has not been possible to do so without creating a fantasy world into which to retreat, freezing the painful emotions, or lashing out in defiance against all and sundry or against particular people in their lives.

They have been craving the security of predictable patterns and responses to their feelings and needs, homely rituals that give a shape to each day—meal time, gathering and bed time. Sadly, however much they have configured and reconfigured the raw material of their lives, it has refused to resemble what they are looking for. Adults like the readers of this book are likely to underestimate the sheer horror and terror that this constantly failing endeavour engenders.

I recall a very gentle, modest game of 'Hide and seek' with two children, aged between 8 and 10, who came to live at Mill Grove. It was one of the few games that they understood, so limited was their sense of rules, games, play and social interaction. The area in which we played was safe and enclosed, with firm boundaries. They hid most often by putting their hands over their eyes and crouching, thus assuming that no one could see them even though there was no physical cover. When I went to hide behind a small shrub, they made a panicky attempt to find me and then both burst into anguished tears. They were obviously terrified, and still recall that game over 15 years later.

The reason for their distress was that, for them, this was not 'just a game' but a real life experience of loss. Desperate for human security, they had not yet internalized any satisfactory attachments.

The same pattern of anxiety and fear recurred in numerous incidents, like the rocking of a boat on a local lake on a fine day, when there was not a breath of air and virtually no ripples on the water, or a walk along a modest cliff path in North Wales, when the two believed they were lost for a very short time. Once again fear engulfed them.[2]

BOUNDARIES AND FREEDOM

For every growing child, not just those with unsatisfactory attachments, there is a constant need for boundaries. These will be provided by nature and the natural world with its days, nights, weeks and seasons; by the social world of parents, families, communities and peer groups; by stories, meals, games and worship; by dance, music and yearly festivals. The opposite of boundaries for a child would be a world where everything was random and unpredictable, where there was no sense of cause and effect, and where they never bumped into anything solid. Sometimes 'freedom' is assumed to be the absence of boundaries. A better understanding would see boundaries as a prerequisite for true freedom. It is the difference between a garden, which is safe bounded space, and a wilderness that stretches in all directions without measurements, familiar landmarks or places of safety.

Where an unattached child lacks a sense of firm and consistent boundaries, he or she is likely to feel out of control and to project this feeling on to others. In such situations, children may well attempt to compensate by trying to control everyone and everything around them (in their 'little world'). It is only as children come to understand and respect their own boundaries that they can begin to accept responsibility for, and therefore take control of, their feelings and behaviour.

Even if we cannot agree on what they should be, we all realize that children need appropriate boundaries—firm without being unduly restrictive.[3] Boundaries that are reasonable can be defended if necessary in a logical and consistent way. They will be sensitive to contemporary changes and needs and to the growing child, and may well be chosen by the child for his or her own children, because they have been experienced as appropriate, proportionate, just and nurturing.

To illustrate the link between boundaries and freedom of expression, I often think about my personal experience of playing the piano. Without the discipline of expert piano lessons, I was floundering with basic concepts and techniques. My piano teacher in Edinburgh stripped me of as many bad habits as she could and went right back to basics. I was told (as someone who had passed Grade 8 years before) to go away and practise the scale of C major, hands separately, one octave. This is the original five-finger exercise on the piano! It is a bit like going from A-level Maths to your two-times table, from gourmet cooking to heating baked beans, or from multi-pitch climbing to a kiddies' climbing frame.

My teacher was determined to get the basics in place before I resumed playing Beethoven sonatas, Bach preludes and fugues and Schubert impromptus—and what were the basic boundaries? Foremost, I realized, was the primacy of listening over the playing of notes, chords and melodies; then there was the position of the body, arm, wrist and fingers—notably the thumb as it curled under the index finger unobtrusively but in such a way that there was no need for wrist movement during the scale. The exercise felt 'degrading' (a very poignant word in light of the exams I had already passed). So what was the point? Simply this: without these basic techniques I would never be able to realize my potential. I would never experience the degree of freedom in my playing that was founded on sound principles.

I went to school with a concert pianist by the name of John Lill. Although we occasionally played pianos together as an accompaniment to the singing of hymns in school assembly, he was in a completely different league from me. He had a solid grounding in classical piano technique, but one of the results is that he can play virtually any type of music: he seems as free as a bird when he sits at a piano.

Despite the attentions of my tutor in Edinburgh, my playing has continued to be very ordinary, but I have found it possible to venture into territory that would have been prohibited had I continued with my very flawed techniques and my inability to listen to and hear the music.

LANGUAGE

Like playing an instrument, ordinary living requires basic boundaries and disciplines. Without them, there can be no language, no social life, no games, no education and no fun. This is not to say that boundaries are themselves entertaining (the example of my piano lessons is intended to be a reminder of this), but that they make everything else possible.

One of the most underrated and neglected of skills is that of language. Whatever language a child learns to speak, and whatever the social class into which they are born,[4] rules of one sort or another are essential to understanding both spoken and signed language as well as to speaking it. These 'rules' are not taught in any formal sense but are communicated by ceaseless repetition of words, phrases and intonations.

In time, the words are used with more complexity of interaction (what we call grammar). No language can exist without boundaries, patterns and shapes, and language will be one of the most important elements in the child's sense of identity and relationships. It always starts with the familiar and then begins to expand. Perhaps it mirrors, and even accompanies and facilitates, the process of oscillation between the secure base and the exploration from that base.

THE DANCE BETWEEN CHILD AND MOTHER

Emotionally there is a language or dance that develops between a mother and her newborn child. It does not involve words (at least, if it does, they are not the primary currency of conversation or intercourse) but, rather, movements and gestures. Within a couple of weeks of birth, there is an emerging set of patterns to this interaction: touch, movement and, crucially, the meeting of eyes, and smiles. All this is beautifully described in Dan Hughes' work.[5]

Janusz Korczak, as he does in so many other aspects of the world of children, gets to the nub of things elegantly, simply and with precision when he talks of the child being able to read the parent's face as adults try to read the weather. He emphasizes that little children spend most of their time doing this, so they are experts in the field. He also talks of a mother and child being able to hold complicated conversations without words.[6]

Now try to imagine a child who cannot predict his parents' mood or reaction to anything, who might be just as easily rewarded or ignored for the same action. Imagine a child who is punished for an action one minute and gets away with it the next. Imagine a child who cannot rely on his parents' word or promises, a child who cannot be sure when the next meal will come, or a child who does not know what objects belong to him or to someone else. What you end up with is a bewildered, frightened, insecure, unhappy, moody and disturbed child.

The difference between chaos and order is not that chaos has storms, tremors, surprises, mistakes and traumas, while order has none. Rather, it is that chaos has, by definition, no boundaries, while order draws from the previous experience or knowledge of boundaries to set current experiences, including trials and testing, in the context of an overall scheme or pattern of things. The young child seeks but does not yet have this sense of pattern and order: it is being established in and through the storms. So, if there is no strong, firm and predictable sense of order ('good enough' experiences of safety), any storm becomes increasingly frightening and out of control.

STORIES AND STORY

Over the years at Mill Grove, I have become increasingly interested in the place that story and stories hold in the lives of developing children.[7] Stories provide very basic categories for understanding self, others and social interaction. Put another way, without a sense of story, a child can have no sense of personal identity or the otherness of others and their identities (the two, of course, go hand in hand). We will come back to this in the next chapter, but for now I would like to stress the place that stories play in the creation of appropriate boundaries.

While teaching a postgraduate degree course in Penang called Holistic Child Development, I hit upon a discovery almost by chance: everyone is a storyteller. I had realized that not everyone was a natural theologian, scientist, poet, writer, parent or organizer, but the universal gift of storytelling appeared as I set a group a particular task, which involved doing biblical exegesis by means of storytelling. This discovery has led me to retrace my steps in an attempt to understand why it is so.

Without going into details about different types of story and genre, we can agree that stories all have a beginning, middle and end, and that there is some link between those elements. The most basic kind of link is in the form of the phrase 'and then'. Life is a mixture of experiences, feelings, events and dreams that we try to make sense of, and the most fundamental way in which we do so is by means of this simple form of narrative or story: 'this... then this... and after that...'.

At the start of life, our storytelling is very limited and patterned: 'I am thirsty, and then I drink'; 'I am frightened, so I cry, and then I am held'—or however we might imagine the primal sequence.

Then the storyline draws in other experiences, and the beginnings of a sense of cause and effect are derived, whether accurate or not. The key to any story is some form of continuity, either in the 'other(s)' or the 'self', or both. I think this may be a fundamental way in which being held sets in train the most rudimentary of autobiographies.

There are various ways in which this developing story can be nurtured: by regular patterns ('I always get held when I am frightened'), by affirmation, by reflection and so on. One of the simplest is by the telling of simple stories—whether using books or not—with the stories repeated time and again, day after day.

There are equally numerous ways in which the emerging story can be disrupted: by individual events or traumas, the scale of which cannot be understood or contained in any way; by unpredictability and lack of any pattern; by deceit, in that promises are made and the goods are not delivered; by fear, or by a stream of experiences that allows no time for assimilation and reflection.[8]

Bedtime stories for children may seem today like a middle-class luxury from a bygone era, but their structuring role may have been undervalued, not just in the sense that they end the day and therefore give pattern to life, but in providing the skeleton of the whole notion of story. 'So Teddy arrived home with a basket of shopping...' was how my favourite story ended. It must have been read to me hundreds of times. Why this demand for repetition if there is no desire for structure and the sense of well-being that comes through a familiar routine?

A question that arises is whether such stories come before the sense of the autobiography of a child or vice versa (and whether language comes before story or vice versa). My interim conclusion is that the two are symbiotic—mutually reinforcing—and I believe that communal rituals and events in which children play a part can be among the most creative and reliable ways in which a sense of story is conveyed. In the context of worship, this means that there is importance not just in the stories that may occur during a church service, but in the sense of story that is the narrative of the worship itself—welcome, event and sending out.

Hidden but essential to this process is listening—the ways in which the child's story is heard, and the ways in which the child learns to listen to the stories of others. The relationship between the storyteller and the listener is one of the primary boundaries in a child's early life. Here, surely, can be traced some of the origins of empathy, sympathy and imagination. If so, we can see the crucial role that story, stories and storytelling play in the emerging boundaries which are vital to the growth of love, with its elemental reciprocity of give and take, tell and listen, surprise and pattern, the unexpected and resolution.

FRÖBEL AND MOVEMENT

Another element in the formation of boundaries concerns not so much time as space. Friedrich Fröbel[9] spent years observing mothers with very young children, and based his theory of human development and learning on one thing: movement. In his kindergarten method he used dance, poetry and actions in which children were grouped in circles rather than placed in rows, sitting at desks.[10] This was an extension of the movement between the mother and very young child—the subtle movements and interactions that Dan Hughes describes as 'dance'.

It is through movement that language is first communicated: stories usually embody some form of movement. Mathematics is based on movement in which things grow (by addition or multiplication) and diminish (by subtraction and division). Geography, in its most elemental form, is not about static maps but about movement in space, which gives a sense of a starting point, a journey and a return. That is how spatial awareness develops, with the crucial sense of distance that is so critical to motor-coordination, safety and relationships.

What has this got to do with boundaries? We discover boundaries by movement, not by conceptualization or thinking. The child feels the mother's breast, touches the mother's face and, in time, bumps into things. There is a very early sense of space, with the impulse to reach out; then come the impulse to crawl and to discover all sorts of relationships in the process, not least the difference between then and now, self and other, here and there.

If we try to imagine a world in which a child can move without any boundaries, we are back to the false concept of 'freedom' that is, in reality, a wilderness of frightening anonymity. Such a universe would be one in which words echoed infinitely into the void, where there was nowhere to aim for and nothing to reach. It would be a bottomless chasm or abyss, a wasteland, a starless, unutterably dark sky. The little child depends on touch, response and reaction. In his or her world, there is the moving object to be picked up, the tiny insect, the cloud that is out of reach, the leaves of the trees moving in the most intricate of patterns, the immovable object, the slippery surface, stickiness, shining, shimmering, the turning of pages, the movement of water in sunlight. Each of these experiences is, whether we notice it or not, dependent on boundaries. Learning is about discovering and (in time) negotiating, forming and internalizing boundaries, and at the very heart of the process is movement between one place and another, one mood and another, one texture and another.

As I have been writing this book, I have been glimpsing everything afresh in and through my grandson, Isaac. In our Greek-influenced world of thought, we stress the distinction between 'this' and 'that' ('A' as distinct from 'non-A'), and delight in static definitions and distinctions. Isaac is an embodiment of movement, interaction and becoming. Each day, what was 'that' (something like riding a tricycle, or bicycle with stabilizers, which others could do but he couldn't) becomes 'this' (something that he can now do himself), and in the process of discovery he often falls off. In fact, I wonder whether there is any way to prevent a little child who has learnt to stand and walk from bumping his head against a table, for example. A book describing what such an encounter might mean in theory would not have the same salutary effect. This is the way we encounter and challenge, or accept and overcome boundaries.

YES AND NO

Possibly more alarming than the first confrontation between the toddling child and something hard and immovable is the startling effect of the first 'No' that he or she hears. Both send immediate messages to the child: one resulting perhaps in shivers down the spine, the other a shuddering of heart and soul. Both are about movement, and both involve boundaries.

For some reason, our contemporary cultures have difficulty with the whole idea of saying 'No' to children. This difficulty may reflect a deep-seated anxiety about negation and death, but, whatever the reason, it creates a huge problem for children, who need to hear 'No' clearly, firmly and consistently spelt out. Strange as it may seem, hearing 'No' is a crucial basis of growth, identity and relationships. It has its place in the growth of love. We may wish to stress the positives of love and loving relationships, but they are built upon ruling out a range of possibilities and options. We will come to this later, but for now let us stay with the importance of 'No' early in the life of the child.

As we have noted, the very young baby cannot distinguish between self and other: everything is part of one indissoluble whole. There is, as yet, no 'A' and 'non-A'. But if self is to develop, such distinctions will need to be made and internalized. If this does not happen, the child is in desperate and constant danger from the realities of the physical world of fire, water, electricity and traffic. All parents accept that there are some situations where a firm 'No' must be said, but we are talking here not simply about protecting the child from danger: there is much more at stake.

This boundary is absolutely fundamental in drawing the distinction between conscious and unconscious, inside and outside, my world and your world. It is by means of the other or non-self that a child has the potential to construct self—the subjective as different from the objective material world. Saying 'No' lays the foundation for subsequent ego development.[11] One of the ways in which children manifest the existence of this process is by saying 'No' themselves, and by blaming 'naughty things' for any harm or displeasure caused. There is a long way to go before the increasing complexity of the world is discovered but at least the attribution of agency to external things shows a recognition that there are things that are 'not me'.

If everything is 'Yes' and pleasurable, the process of self-development is retarded. Anxiety and separation are vital for psychic growth and health. This is dangerous ground, for there is the ever-present possibility that the boundaries will be unwisely drawn, for whatever reason, by the child or others, which may lead to unhealthy repression and trauma. In reaction to that possibility, we may decline to affirm the 'No', but this is not a good way to proceed for the child's sake. Healthy repression is a necessary part of development. This is counter-intuitive but on reflection it is seen to be true.

The religious faith of parents and family, and the community of which they are part, may enable them to be firm in saying 'No' because they know that negation, anxiety and death are not only not the end (and therefore to be feared above all things) but are the very basis of creative life and relationships. They believe in the ultimate order and harmony of things. The 'face' of God is always reassuring, however stern the realities of life may be. Given that for the little child, here and now is everywhere and eternity, and the family and home are the whole world, it matters greatly whether this world is to be trusted. The child will be able to read deep into the heart and emotions of the adults in his or her life, to detect whether trust outweighs mistrust for them.

As the child grows in understanding of the physical and social world around him or her, part of what is going on is the establishing of moral boundaries—what is acceptable and unacceptable in the child's social group (kingdom); what is desirable and undesirable; what is praised and what is reprimanded. The child's growing desire for autonomy provides the movement that inevitably results in such clashes, and the nature and management of these moral boundaries varies greatly from continent to continent and time to time. At the back of them all, however, is some form of the 'Golden Rule' ('Do to others as you want them to do to you'), which assumes that some things belong to another person or group and some things belong to the child.

BOUNDARIES: CLEAR, CONSISTENT AND LIVED

It is not the intention of this book to provide a set of definitions of right and wrong for the growing child, or a manual of the ways in which these definitions should be introduced. It is my purpose, however, to describe how important they are, and what my experience has taught me. A basic rule of thumb is that the boundaries must be clear, consistent, and lived. Let me unpack these principles briefly.

However many 'grey areas' there may be in real life for the adults who have responsibility for the growing child, it is not helpful for the child to be left, like Hamlet, in a state of constant bewilderment and quandary. Boundaries must be clear to all concerned, so parents need to make it abundantly obvious that their 'Yes' is 'Yes', and their 'No' is 'No'. The half-no, or the taken back 'no' is not only confusing but also debilitating for the child. It represents a weakness to the child, when the child actually requires something firm.[12] The sooner the child accepts the simple fact that the parent means what is said, the better for her security and exploration, for she can start exploring in a new and more informed way from that point on. Without that acceptance, there will be a tendency to stick at this point and to continue testing it—

for example, saying, 'Can I have some more sweets?' again and again.

I recall a time when a boy whose family we were supporting over many years was with us for lunch. He was beginning to become unsettled, which was affecting everyone in the room. Very quietly and gently I told him that he should stop whatever he was doing. He ignored me and continued his behaviour in a way obvious to all around, so I informed the rest of the family that the boy and I needed to talk by ourselves. We left the table at my insistence and we walked along the street towards his family house.

He was upset and no doubt worried about what I might say to his parents. They were not in, so we continued to talk to each other. His basic argument was that I had been unfair because I had not given him a second chance. He continued, 'My mum always gives me another chance!' That was it in a nutshell: he was used to people shouting at him again and again, whereas I had not done so. 'It's unfair!' was not just a summary of the situation but a cry from his heart.

(We notice, in passing, the difficulty of a child seeking to reconcile differing boundaries between the constituent parts of his world.) We walked quietly back to Mill Grove and I sought to reassure him that whenever he was with me, he could rely on the fact that if I said 'Yes' I meant 'Yes', and the same with 'No'. There was no more to be said on the subject: it would be pointless to pursue it. (I ought to add that increasingly since then, as he has grown up, I have often told him that I am unsure and don't know, or need more time to think about an issue.)

There is little doubt in my mind that this one occasion laid the foundations for a significant and positive change in our relationship. We have been able to move on, at meal times, in games and in conversation. We enjoy each other's company and there is mutual respect. I was telling him to stop something—it was a 'No', and that was unpleasant for both of us—but the greater significance was that it established a clear boundary for him, and also reinforced one that was understood by the rest of our family. It was not arbitrary, of course—not a boundary for the sake of a boundary. It was necessary in my judgment, and it had significance for the whole of our relationship.

Saying 'No' is neither easy nor trouble-free but once we see the importance of boundaries in a child's life, we will appreciate the critical role of boundary setting and maintenance. In the physical world, wood will remain wood, fire will remain fire, day will be day, night will be night, and gravity will operate in a downwards direction. That is reassuring for the child and for parents, as it means the child is always getting some consistent messages day by day. But moral boundaries are for us to establish in the context of our social world and time.

Boundaries must be not only clear but consistent, which means that those parenting the child must agree on certain things—and this parenting, as you already know, includes teachers and others in the child's growing kingdom. Children will inevitably test boundaries again and again, so they must be firm and reliable. For this reason, proposed boundaries must be carefully considered and then conscientiously and quietly maintained. I stress the word 'quietly'. Shouting and temper have no place in establishing moral boundaries. They are likely to produce the opposite effect to the one intended, and will usually indicate that boundaries are fragile or not agreed.

While boundaries need to be firm and unyielding, at the same time there must be appropriate flexibility. This is very difficult to describe—a flexible but unyielding boundary seems like a contradiction in terms—but the paradox is intuitively grasped by 'good enough' parents and teachers. There must be some 'give' in the boundaries, which means that they are not so hard that they injure those who encounter them. At the same time, although there is some give, there is never any question about the fact that the boundary will hold. This element of boundary-keeping by adults is a lifelong art involving humour, good judgment and personal relationships.

A third important quality of boundary making, marking and maintenance is that moral boundaries should be lived. In describing Mill Grove, I often point out that we do not have a list of rules because we try to establish our boundaries by 'living' them, so that the child learns to observe and, in time, mirror the behaviour of parents and significant adults. This is far from easy. In organizations that care for children, there should be clear accountability, allowing the carer the authority and space to live boundaries rather than relaying rules to the children for whom they are responsible.[13]

The need for forgiveness and restoration is implicit in the process of establishing and maintaining moral boundaries, because the fact is that people transgress boundaries. If there is no way back, no way of reintegration into the accepted group and way of doing things, boundaries will be a source of inordinate fear.[14] This is all so very far from the Christian gospel that we might wonder about the social sources of religious denominationalism: there must always be the hope of forgiveness in the growing child.

HOME AND (PRE)SCHOOL

At some point in the lives of most children, there is a physical relocation between home and nursery or school, and this is a critical point in their development. At whatever age it happens, the child has become accustomed to a set of patterns and norms, to sounds, smells, people and interactions, and now a new world beckons. The management of these two worlds is a challenge to parents and teachers, and to the child (who, after all, is the only one who actually has to live in both worlds). While it is impossible and probably undesirable that these two worlds should be perfectly matched and interwoven, it is important that they should have enough in common to ensure that the young child's sense of security, story and boundaries is not undermined. In this process, transitional objects, common patterns and people who know each other all have a part to play.

Perhaps I am laying emphasis here because of my own experience of this rite of passage. I did not go to a preschool nursery, so the first day at primary school was a traumatic experience for me. I have never been able to make a conscious link, but the fact that I was abandoned in hospital at the age of three for an operation to remove my tonsils[15] almost certainly contributed to my sense of abandonment on the first day of new school. My mother took me on her bicycle, and spent time with me in the playground until a bell rang. Then she said goodbye, got on her bicycle and, for the first time that I could remember, set off, ignoring my increasingly desperate cries for her to come back.

I still recall that exact moment. It was tinged with complete disbelief and a sense of loss and possibly betrayal. Compared to the experience of others, the rest of my school career was relatively peaceful and successful, but I don't think anyone (whether at home or school) ever understood the angst and loneliness that I felt on that day. I guess the experience has coloured subsequent moves, too, including the first term away from home at university. It is a partial tribute to the work of Bowlby and others that we have come to realize that there are better ways of managing the boundaries between home and school.[16]

GAMES

We will return to the subject of games in Chapter Seven, but it is vital to see their part in the creation and maintenance of boundaries. I am not saying that this is their purpose—or 'learning outcome', to quote a contemporary mantra—but that this is both what happens when children play and a prerequisite for any game to take place.

You will remember the two little children who cried when I was hiding during that game of hide and seek. It will not require a great feat of imagination to realize that one of them might have had difficulty in playing other games. On the same day, she played a game of snakes and ladders. Each time she rolled the dice, she changed it so that the six was facing up. This meant that she could throw again, and so she inevitably won the game. In fact, there could be no game, because her opponent never had a chance to throw. When this practice was gently and carefully challenged by an experienced social worker, the child tipped the board over, spilling counters and dice everywhere, and stormed off. It was several years before she could accept the boundaries that you and I think of as the 'rules of the game', yet without these boundaries, what hope was there for the rest of her life as she interacted with people? What sort of childhood is it without games and play?

In my submission, the significance of play in the development of children cannot be stressed too highly. I am thinking of every possible sort of game: formal and informal, inside and out, board games and playground games. They involve many of the elements of social life and interaction vital for the development of a child's moral understanding and capacity. Little noticed, perhaps, is the way roles are often reversed in games: in a board game you may play alternately black or white; in hide and seek the players take it in turns to hide. This is simple and yet profound, for here is the fundamental essence of role play—the process of assuming a role for a time and, more importantly, recognizing that the other player is also playing a role and respecting that role.

We see here the emerging process of understanding self and others. Part of this process is precisely the ability to imagine oneself away from self to the concept of a generalized 'other'. This may sound like a small step but, given that the newborn child does not distinguish in any way between self and anything else, it marks great progress in identity formation and social development.

SEXUALITY

Sexuality is integral to the lives of children and adolescents. They are as inquisitive about sexual organs and sexual behaviour as about every other aspect of their lives and world, and exploration and experimentation are natural. So what about sexual boundaries?[17]

What I have written so far about boundaries must incorporate sexuality, but I would like to explore in a little more detail the influence of global media on children and childhood. My conviction is that the media are of great and growing importance in every area of children's lives, but I will discuss their influence in relation to sexuality. Present and future generations of children live in a new type of environment, where they are increasingly connected to aspects of the world 'directly' through electronic communication rather than through the mediation of parents, families and teachers. This opens up new possibilities for learning and exploration, but the flip side is that commercialism, through advertising and consumerism, is targeting these children for its own economic purposes.

When introducing the notion of boundaries into this equation, we find that societies are either very slow or impotent in the face of this threat to some aspects of childhood. How does a family provide informed and appropriate censorship (yes, there is no running away from this reality) of the images that will otherwise stream into the child's consciousness? 24-hour television channels and the growing availability of the internet mean that the creation and maintenance of these boundaries by parents (that is, 'villagers') may be one of the greatest challenges of our times.

As one who travels quite widely, I have been struck by the pleas of caring adults on every continent for help in protecting their children from 'Western' media. They tell of the ways in which childhood is wrenched away from the poor children in their countries by the premature sexualization to which they are exposed. Our talk of 9 o'clock watersheds doesn't mean a lot around the world. This is an area where I feel that churches and faith communities should take a lead: the economics of the process, and the idea of liberty so dear to Western democracies, mean that governments find it hard to know whether or how to intervene.

Why is it that our contemporary societies are so hard on individual child abusers but so weak and feeble when it comes to corporate paedophiles? If it takes a village to parent—and it is now true that we live in a global village—it surely behoves multinational media corporations to consider how they can join the rest of us in considerate, informed and sensitive parenting, at whatever level of involvement.

One of the issues for children in relation to sexuality is the awareness of what is personal or private and what is to be shared with others. This is a matter of conversation, clothing, behaviour, touch and so on, and it is, of course, something that changes with the changing years. The so-called private parts of each person are not very private when nappies are regularly being changed, but they are much more personal in the emerging adult. It is essential that children receive reasonably consistent boundaries in this, as in other matters of daily living. My sense is that today the messages are likely to be very confusing for many children. I think, for example, of teenagers in Muslim families living in the United Kingdom, and wonder how they forge a sensible path through the competing messages and diametrically opposed norms all around them.

BOUNDARIES IN THE BIBLE

We turn now to see how the scriptures enlighten and inform us on the subject of boundaries. As with the theme of security, we find that we have struck a rich vein, both literally and symbolically.

We saw in Chapter Three how the biblical story tells of places that have clear and reassuring boundaries: the garden of Eden, Noah's ark, the promised land, Jerusalem and the new Jerusalem. There are also symbolic boundaries that speak of safety: Abraham's bosom, fortresses, city walls, the place that Jesus promised to prepare for his disciples, the family and community of God. Then there are moral boundaries represented by detailed laws, summarized in the Ten Commandments.

The division between the sacred and profane is critical to all religions, however much people may differ about their definitions of where the division lies and how it applies. The people at the foot of the trembling, smoking Mount Sinai were warned not to come too near; the camp plan during the wilderness years made clear how close people should come to the tent that contained the ark of the covenant; the temple replicated this sense of safe distance between a holy God (the Holy of Holies) and the people (the Court of the Gentiles); Moses and the prophets knew that it was vital to acknowledge the holiness of God by recognizing holy ground and taking off their shoes. 'Don't come near me! I am a sinner', is a refrain in the Bible in several variations (see, for example, Luke 5:8). Much of the Old Testament law deals with the interface between the religious and everyday worlds, and in the New Testament there is the developing theme of whether and how much the Jewish law is to be applied in Christian homes and communities: the wine of the new covenant cannot be contained within the boundaries (the wineskins) of the old, for example (Luke 5:37).

For the growing child getting to grips with the Bible narrative from an early age, there are descriptions of people wrestling with moral boundaries: what is right and wrong; what is praised and decried and so on. So Adam and Eve transgress a moral boundary and suffer the consequences of being expelled from the safety of the garden of Eden; the people of Noah's time are disobedient and find themselves excluded from the ark.[18] In the book of Exodus, the Egyptians respond differently to God's instructions and the result is plagues, while the Israelites are kept safe by the blood of the lamb on their doorposts and lintels. The stories of the entry into the promised land, and of the kings of Israel and Judah, are set in a clear moral context: some kings do what is pleasing in the sight of God and are blessed as a result, while others do what is displeasing and, in time, evil results.

Among the most neglected resources in the Christian heritage for the establishment of moral boundaries in families and communities are the Ten Commandments. For 20 years or so, I have pleaded with congregations of different denominations to have one Sunday service a year, at least, when children are present, at which they present all of the Ten Commandments. Many churches never mention any of the commandments but those that do always opt for the 'summary of the law': 'Love the Lord your God with all your heart, soul, strength, and mind' and 'Love others as much as you love yourself' (Luke 10:27; Matthew 22:39). The main reason church leaders give for this decision is that there isn't time in the service to read through all Ten Commandments. The time given to different activities always represents a view of priorities and, to me, the priorities revealed are staggeringly inappropriate.

What does it mean that churches will not present the Ten Commandments? I have concluded reluctantly that they assume we know them already, or that it is of no particular advantage to children and young people to know them. In my view, this is a disastrous and comprehensive, if not wilful, misreading of the situation. These boundaries (which we might usefully consider as 'the Maker's instructions') are a heritage of priceless worth. We spurn them at the peril of our children and our children's children.

The prophets constantly wrestled with moral challenges and dilemmas. Isaiah (perhaps representative of the Old Testament prophets) describes a dramatic shaking of taken-for-granted boundaries, starting with conventional understandings of religious worship, and stating that God gets tired of it all unless it is prefaced by the seeking of justice and the care of those who are weak and poor (1:10–17). The divisions between 'them' and 'us' are challenged and, when he describes the day of the Lord and the new Jerusalem, many things seem inside out (56:3–8).

Most people, whether Christians or not, would recognize in the life and teaching of Jesus Christ some of the most profoundly relevant, inspiring and challenging moral examples and teachings of all time. His boundaries were clear, consistent and lived, to use the phrase employed earlier in this chapter. The Sermon on the Mount sets out the received commandments of the old covenant and redefines them to the point where they seem impossible to keep. The kingdom of heaven is subversive of traditional ways of living and organization; those who are outcast are welcome; the parables turn accepted values on their heads, and the concept of family is redefined.

Kristin Herzog makes the telling point that God in Christ kept within boundaries: 'Jesus' life mirrors God's self-emptying, keeping within the boundaries of what is truly human.'[19]

ENCOUNTERING BIBLICAL BOUNDARIES

These boundaries, original and redefined, are often set in the stories and accounts of events that we find in the Bible. This means that children hearing (and later reading) the stories, poetry and prophecy are called into an active relationship with them. It becomes clear that they present practical moral choices and dilemmas.

Critical in this process is the way in which the boundaries are perceived, learned and then internalized. I have had the privilege in recent years of listening to children respond to Bible stories and themes during sessions of Godly Play.[20] Integral to the storytelling is the way the adult facilitator creates a safe space (boundaries) in which the children can explore, reflect and discuss issues without the danger of censure or, for that matter, praise. The problem in the case of the former is obvious; in the case of the latter, the risk is that the children will always be trying to find the 'right' answer as far as the adult is concerned, rather than the morally correct answer for themselves.

On one occasion, I was present as part of a group hearing the story of the Ten Commandments. The commandments were visible on a little piece of rock as the narrative unfolded. They were then compared with the teaching of Jesus about loving our enemies. A lively discussion ensued, in which one of the children insisted that this was going too far. It was bad enough trying to love his sister all the time, let alone his enemies. He made it very clear that if this was demanded of Christians, then the game was up for him. He simply couldn't fulfil its expectations or demands. His sister agreed that there was a fundamental problem here.

The group then discussed examples of how Jesus' teaching contradicted what had happened in European history—for example, in the Second World War, when Christians had actually killed (rather than loved) their enemies. It wasn't long before the discussion spread out to include current events and the moral teaching of other world faiths, notably Islam. What about suicide bombings? Did the Koran teach anything about loving enemies? The facilitator allowed the discussion to continue without anything more than points of clarification or affirmation, and I was left with a sense that the children had taken part in a process that was so much more mature and relevant than what happens in most sermons and Bible studies for adults.

Societies around the world and through time have found ways of passing their moral and religious values, stories, precepts and patterns on to the next generations, and the Christian story is one of many. I can say from experience over many years that the Bible is a remarkable source of material for this purpose in many ways, not least the way in which it invites the reader or listener to become part of the overall story. The child's story intersects in time with the biblical narrative.

There is a telling refrain in the Pentateuch and early history books of the Jewish scriptures: 'When your children ask you… then tell them…' (Exodus 12:26–27; Joshua 4:6–7). This is a key to the whole process. It includes the matter of the timing of the moral lesson, the initiative of the child, and the response to the question, but the context for all this is the regular celebration of events. It is worship that provides the context for the questions and the subsequent retelling of the story.

Family life, daily living and yearly rhythms and events will always provide rich opportunities for the process of passing values on to the next generation. Faith schools, committed Christian families and faith communities alike have a wonderful resource in the Bible and the worship and gatherings of which children are a part. I am not sure how the imparting of values is handled by those of no particular faith or cultural community; doubtless there are good resources and models. Without decrying them in any way, I continue to be amazed and humbled by the nature and quality of the Christian heritage about 'teaching children how they should live' (Proverbs 22:6, GNB).[21]

SUMMARY

Starting from the boundaries necessary for a child to experience safety and security, we have moved into the realm of moral boundaries. Using the word 'boundaries' rather than the narrower term 'discipline' has allowed a range of comparisons and connections to be made. A growing child moves between various social groups, and the boundaries within each, and between them, all have a part to play in providing the context in which love can grow.

❖

Chapter Five

SIGNIFICANCE

Can a mother forget the baby at her breast and have no compassion on the child she has borne? Though she may forget, I will not forget you! See, I have engraved you on the palms of my hands.

Isaiah 49:15–16 (NIV)

SELF AND OTHERS

We come to the third and central of the themes or motifs in our five-finger exercise. The words that would be most commonly used as alternatives for 'significance' are probably 'confidence', 'self-worth', 'identity' or 'ego'. The focus of this theme is the emerging sense of 'me' or 'myself' in the growing child. Erik Erikson refers to the 'organisation of experience in the individual ego... a sense of coherent individuation and identity: of being one's self, of being all right'.[1] There can be no love, with the giving and receiving of affection, promises, tenderness, and sacrifice mentioned already, unless there is a genuine belief or assumption first that 'I am', and second that 'I' matter or am worth something to myself or to anyone else.

Trust is often associated with trusting something or someone else, but a fundamental and understated element is trust of our self—both to control our own urges and to cope with the challenges that come our way.[2] Jesus put it simply and with great insight when he affirmed the commandment, 'Love others as much as you love yourself' (Matthew 22:39). Love for others cannot exist without roots in a 'good enough' experience of self.

This self cannot grow in isolation. It develops in and through relationships. This has been expressed in many ways, but the words of the sociologists Peter and Brigitte Berger are particularly memorable: 'Only by internalising the words of others can we speak to ourselves. If no one had significantly addressed us from the outside, there would be silence within ourselves as well. It is only through others that we discover ourselves.'[3] There is throughout life, but particularly in the childhood years, a continuous negotiation between, on the one hand, how I feel about myself, who I believe I am and what I want to be and, on the other, how others see, describe and label me. Some of this negotiation is conscious and deliberately contested, but much of it is unconscious.[4]

G.H. Mead usefully suggests the use of the word 'me' to represent how others see (that is, label, categorize and value) a person, and the word 'I' for how that person sees him- or herself.[5] It is helpful to have two separate words to describe the interaction between the internal version of who I believe myself to be and the external version of the person others deem or assume me to be. In order for a consistent internalized sense of self to emerge, the input, affirmation and nurture of significant others is important, yet these others will not simply go along with the wishes and views of the child, but will challenge, affirm and seek to refine the 'I'. Sensitive others will not overwhelm or exasperate the child to the point where he or she gives up the negotiation by the mechanisms of fight (that is, to contest everything) or flight (that is, to withdraw into a shell).

Where there is little space for the individual sense of identity and worth of a child to grow, the risk of mental illness is high.[6] In an oppressive and inescapable situation, the child has little option but to split off from it and create an imaginary or fantasy world. The discourse that is made up of the many ways in which parents and children relate to one another has dried up, and the significance of the child is now no longer affirmed by the relationship. Whether the fantasy world will be able to enable the child to develop as an adult in relation to the rest of the social world is an open question, but the risk that it will not is considerable.

UNCONDITIONAL COMMITMENT

My clinical experience tends to confirm the principle that, in order for a healthy sense of self to develop, there must be one other person on earth who is totally and unconditionally committed to me as an individual for a significant part of my life. By 'unconditionally' I mean that nothing I do will affect that commitment; I do not have to behave in a prescribed or positive way to maintain it. I do not have to deserve affection and love. They are simply a fact, non-negotiable and rock-like.

With the recognition that death will interrupt the most committed and loyal relationships, and that the realities of life will present conflicting loyalties of place and responsibility, this statement needs a little clarification. I do not mean that the committed person will effectively halt his or her own life and give complete and undivided attention to a child 24 hours a day and for the whole of life. What I mean is that the child will know that he or she is 'engraved', as it were, on the heart of a significant adult, and that nothing by way of unpleasant behaviour or distance can disturb this commitment. It is what writers like Bowlby and Anna Freud mean by 'mother-love'.

The roots of this love for most people are, of course, found in the bonds established between a biological parent and his or her baby. It is expected that the mother or father of a child will normally remain unconditionally committed (that is, will continue to be loving parents), whatever happens to the child, throughout childhood and the teenage years. For many children, however, there is no such person. Where this is so, it is my view that the primary task of all who seek to help a child at risk—in need, vulnerable, or whatever term we use—is to identify a significant adult as a non-negotiable priority and then to introduce this person to the child in such a way that bonding is given every possible chance.

We are talking here about a personal relationship that has nothing to do with labels and systems of care. It is based on genuine understanding, respect and affection. It is therefore not possible to substitute another person in the relationship. It has nothing to do with case files or groups and carers; it is about a person who knows a child by name and is known to the child by name. Both parties believe the other person to be of incalculable importance. The significant other delights in the child: it is not about calculated intervention and rational analysis so much as the joy of being together. It is about genuine and spontaneous reactions, not so much to particular events, words or products as to the soul and inner being of the child. There is no short cut to the soul of any person, so time is of the essence, and covenant-type commitment is the guarantor that the time will be available and respected.

I know this issue is very challenging, and people have responded to me on it with many comments and strong feelings, but nothing I have encountered in over 30 years among hurting children has done anything to shake my faith in the importance of unconditional commitment in the lives of children. I believe that, in many ways, the education and so-called 'care' systems simply tinker with helping children in need, satisfying the adult need for assurance that something is being done rather than getting to the root of the matter, so I am calling for a fundamental review of our priorities and policies. Much emphasis has been placed on the issue of 'child protection' in recent years, but is there a better way of ensuring the safety and well-being of a child than by having someone who is unconditionally committed to their welfare?

Adoption (a term used carefully and specifically in the Bible to describe how, through Christ, a person becomes a member of God's family and can call him 'Abba') is a logical outworking of this principle where a child has no surviving relatives committed to his or her welfare. For all its difficulties, it is one of the ways of demonstrating to children the fact that there are those who are unconditionally committed to them. A related biblical term is *goel* or 'kinsman-redeemer'. The story that illustrates this relationship most vividly is the story of Ruth and Boaz (Ruth 2:1—4:13), in which we find that there is someone on earth who has responsibility for Naomi's family.

We can use what term we feel to be most appropriate in our current settings, but the crucial element of the role of *goel* is that there is no way of escaping the obligation. Expressed from the other point of view, the person in need knows that the *goel* can be relied upon completely. It seems to me that at Mill Grove, where actual legal adoption has been rare, we are seen over time in the role of 'kinsmen-redeemers' by many of the children, even though they may not know the term.

The commitment, in our case, is lifelong. Long after the children have grown up and set off to different parts of the world, they have no hesitation in contacting us when they are in need of help, comfort or counsel. I have just read a letter from one of the Mill Grove family living in Chicago, who has recently lost his wife. He writes of the comfort it is to know that we are always 'there', and that is what this significance means. You know that wherever you may be in relation to the other person geographically, it makes no difference to the relationship and commitment between you. It doesn't have to be 'warmed up' or kept alive: it simply is; it can be taken for granted. There is no need for the least anxiety or worry about it, so it is a source of peace.

Such commitment is the prerequisite for satisfactory attachment experience and behaviour. When the bond is internalized, there is no longer any need for the adult actually to be there: the fact remains that the adult will always hold the child in their heart. It is not something that can be switched on and off; it simply is, or is not, there. That is what is meant by the word 'unconditional'.

Relationships will encounter testings and storms, and this is what reveals their quality. Much of the task of childhood is to test out relationships in order to see if they are genuine, sensitive and responsive, and this is particularly so in the case of children who have known separation and loss. They dare not replicate the trust of their former relationship and the risk of subsequent pain and so will instinctively push away and reject a person who expresses care and affection. The understanding and commitment of such an adult are tested to the limit.

Having established the strength of an unconditional relationship, it is possible for a child to begin to trust other people and groups as part of the process of the growing self. Extended families, communities, peer groups, schools and teachers, faith groups and societies then can reinforce the sense of worth.

The story Jesus told of a father and his two sons (Luke 15:11–32) describes the essence of unconditional love. The younger son does not merit his father's love (no one contests this in the story), but although he plans to ask to be made a hired servant, he still calls his loving parent 'Father'. Whatever he may have done does not change the fact that they are related as father and son, and the father's reaction shows that the relationship is not just about legal or biological connections: the father continues to love his son. This love has not withered or been adversely affected because of absence or irresponsible behaviour. The father loves his son unconditionally.

THE ABSENCE AND UNDERMINING
OF UNCONDITIONAL COMMITMENT

What are the signs that this commitment is absent or doubted? I wonder whether we have given labels to all sorts of syndromes and conditions that can be traced, to some extent, to the anxiety or fear proceeding from the lack of unconditional commitment in childhood. I don't think that symptoms work in a mechanical or mechanistic way. Life's many variations, individual personalities and events, and the unconscious mind conspire (or protect) against this.

If unconditional commitment is lacking, not only is the development of genuine trust undermined; all the ills associated with the absence of boundaries can also be seen, for this commitment forms one of the most vital boundaries in life. Where trust is absent, the formation of other relationships becomes very difficult. A child tries to win or buy friendship and favour, and doubts that displays of affection or affirmation by others are genuine. The likelihood is that the resulting anxiety will lead to an unhealthy desire to please and conform, or to a willingness to manipulate people and control situations. Nothing is secure, so everything must be cultivated, maintained, encouraged, bought or earnt.

Objects and routines will tend to fill the place of this lack—for example, clothes and the importance attached to appearance, rather than the self-assurance that comes from knowing we are valued by someone else, whatever we look like. There is also likely to be a lifelong search for substitutes for the committed person, perhaps in pornography and sexual relationships, in work, in regressive and infantile religious faith, or in hobbies and interests.

It is my view that much contemporary social behaviour makes sense in the light of this situation. I am not arguing that the condition is more or less common than in previous eras, but that we may be disguising its importance by using other terms of diagnosis and treatment. Before we launch into more detailed theories and experiments, perhaps we should concentrate on this factor, from which so much flows and on which so much depends.

One of the practical applications of the belief that it 'takes a village to parent' is that the need to provide unconditional commitment applies to all of us who have anything to do with the lives of children. It is not possible to predict what demands such a commitment will make. It does not mean that a person will necessarily give up everything for a child, but it does entail a conscious commitment to be there without strings attached.[7] A teacher, grandparent, uncle, aunt, godparent or friend may fulfil this role. I am not sure if it can be fulfilled by a group of people such as a church fellowship, religious community or local authority 'corporate parent'. I sense that it must be an individual, whatever valuable functions groups may play in parenting.

Although I have dealt with the matter in more detail in other lectures and papers,[8] brief mention is appropriate here of alternative forms of parenting—adoption, foster care and residential care. They each have their own strengths and weaknesses, and none of them should be seen as a panacea for all children's ills. Children may find unconditional commitment in any of them or none; it depends on the child and his or her story. It also depends on the wider context—such as, for example, conditions of famine, war and disease in parts of Africa, which make rigid dogmatic declarations by others seem not only strangely out of touch but also redolent of a bygone colonial era.

Whatever system is used, we must not duck the critical issue of identifying a person who is unconditionally committed to each child. A question that constantly surfaces concerns the number of children to whom a single person can be unconditionally committed. There is a general sense that in a small group of, say, ten children, it may be possible, but that in a group of 100 or more, it is not. My studies have led me to doubt whether it is possible to set limits.

It may be that the question is best raised from the other point of view: with how many other children can a child share the sense of being of special significance to a loved and loving adult? There is probably no limit to the number of children for whom an adult can function in this role. Thus, residential care like that of Pandita Ramabai, Herbert White and others may well provide just this commitment, while in foster care a child may experience a number of breakdowns and changes of placements. In either case, the primary task is to identify a person and to facilitate or nurture the relationship between the child and that person.

Institutionalization is another matter, not completely divorced from the issue of significance but neither to be mistaken as the same thing. I share the concern over institutions and institutionalization worldwide (having seen many institutions from the inside), but at the same time there seems to be another factor at work: whereas a mother (or substitute) can be unconditionally committed by providing breast milk to only two children at a time, it is possible for potentially hundreds of older children to relate symbolically to a mother or father figure. When the leader of a nation dies, it sometimes reveals a bonding that might have been overlooked in this context.

One of the most important roles of the kinsman-redeemer is in combating all bullying that undermines the significance and self-worth of children. It has been a constant responsibility for me throughout my time at Mill Grove, and it requires determination and persistence. The persecution of individual children has gone on for time immemorial, but now electronic communication means that there is nowhere safe for many children to hide, as they suffer 24-hour exposure to critical messages from an unlimited number of people. This means that bullying is more difficult to trace and root out in some of its more insidious forms.

Bullying appears in many guises worldwide, from child soldiering, the rape and sex trafficking of young children, and the domination of religious parents, to the labelling and ostracising of a child by a peer group. Labelling affects many children, including girls, those with physical and mental disabilities, homosexuals, those from a different religion or ethnic group, those with unusual habits, and those from despised backgrounds. In every case, bullying attacks the self-worth of children and undermines their sense of being accepted and significant. Despite the fact that schools in the UK have anti-bullying policies and seek to encourage awareness of bullying, many still do not take it seriously enough or realize its scale and pervasiveness. All those who assume parenting roles need to be aware of this issue.[9]

All these things have in common the despising of particular children or groups of children, and the use of the word 'despise' is of particular significance for Christians. In Matthew 18:10, with a little child beside him, Jesus warned his disciples not to 'despise [look down on] one of these little ones' (NRSV). We need to reflect carefully on the scope and intensity of this despising in its many and varied forms in our contemporary world, including advertising, cyberbullying and the sexual grooming of children on the internet. If we take Jesus seriously, we will seek both to show how significance and self-worth in children can be affirmed and to warn about anything that hinders them.

LIFE STORIES

Where there is unconditional commitment, it is inevitable that over time the child and adult will come to know the other's story. Life stories are integral to the process of the growth of self, for we are part of our stories and our stories are part of us. Where two people are 'in love', it is natural for them to seek to learn the other's story. Indeed, it could be argued that one aspect of lifelong marriage is the opportunity it gives for each partner to learn more of the life of the other. If a life story includes trauma, it may take much time and trust before a person is able and willing to share it with the other.

Even as I write this, I have been looking at some photos of my wife, aged between three and six, that I had never seen before (after 37 years of knowing each other). Others might study her photos and life story as part of a social or psychological history, but I love to hear the memories associated with them because they add to my knowledge of the object of my love. My curiosity in turn causes her to remember more. I have visited many of the places important to her in her childhood and met many of the people who helped to shape her life. The story goes way back to before she was born—to her family tree and her roots—and our relationship makes all this personally important. Time past, in this way, is made present for us now.[10]

Human beings have a psychological and social desire to trace and draw from their roots. I am struck by how often those who have been adopted, or have grown up separated from their biological families and communities, are not only desperately isolated and alone, but also feel that they are 'nobodies'. I recall someone aged over 75 saying to me, after having discovered and met one of his relatives whom he had never known, 'Now I am somebody.' I also remember a young woman in a similar situation who, on giving birth to a baby, told me, 'Now I am somebody.' Drawing from roots and establishing roots for the next generation are integral to the whole notion of life stories.

One of the most harmful aspects of the loss of parents and home (and there are many) is the loss of one's personal story and identity. Much of our own story resides in the memories and artefacts that carry special meanings and associations, including such things as particular rooms, chairs, toys, carpets, trees or crockery.

Someone who is unconditionally committed to another will want to learn the life story of that other person. A life story is not just a series of events that a child can remember and retell: it is a way of describing the whole world of the child.[11] To a listening adult it might seem as if the child's story is but a small part of the whole world. After all, this child is but one of millions spread across the world. As a parallel, we might think of the story of the human race on earth: it is about what happens on a very unimportant ball of matter that might just as well be considered as a speck of dust among the 200 million galaxies of the universe, each containing perhaps 200 billion stars.[12] Yet human beings on this earth see their emergence and history as significant—if not to the rest of the universe, at least to them. So it is with the story of the child: it might as well be about everything, because in early childhood it is the whole story and covers everything of any significance to that child.

Stories require a teller and a listener. Without witnesses, a story might just as well be a series of sounds signifying nothing. So the person who hears the child's story is not just a listener to a narrative but a witness to the whole world of the child; and where the witness has his or her emotional and moral eyes open, the unfolding world of the young child is a cause of wonder. The discoveries and the progress are remarkable—not just in the case of child prodigies, but in most children. I often have the privilege of listening to parents of children with cerebral palsy, telling me about the progress that their children are making. Somehow they speak with a greater sense of joy and wonder than many parents of children considered as 'normal'.

One of the people who has taught me most about the place of life story in committed relationships is Pandita Ramabai. Between 1890 and 1922, she cared for up to 2000 orphans and abandoned girls in her Christian community near Poona in India, and she not only knew all their names but had listened to their stories. She was able to write them down or tell them to others. In some cases it had taken many hours, if not days, before a girl felt able to share her experiences with someone else for the first time.[13]

A more recent example of a person who listened to the stories of children comes from the Philippines. Joey Velasco painted a picture of the Last Supper, taking Leonardo da Vinci's great work of art as his model, but replacing the disciples with children whom he had met and photographed in the slums in and around Manila. The picture is now famous. While I was in Manila in the last months of 2006, it was being shown in one of the biggest shopping malls of the capital, and receiving great acclaim. But Joey found himself becoming more disturbed and eventually he decided, for reasons unclear to himself, to seek out each of the children afresh. This he did, and managed to trace them all.

He then wrote a book, *They Have Jesus*,[14] in which he describes how he sat with each of the children and listened to them telling him their stories. He also provided them with much-needed food and drink, but the greatest significance of the encounters was the fact that these children found someone who really desired them to trust him with their real stories. Now they are not only in a famous painting but in a popular book, and so they are reminded of their significance in two ways, but there is little doubt in my mind that the actual encounter between the artist and each child will prove of most lasting significance to them. He wanted nothing more, nothing less, than to hear their stories: they meant everything to him.

Listening to someone's life story no doubt does and means many things, but one of them (as these examples illustrate) is that it gives the storyteller a sense of significance. I believe I am a 'nobody'—nobody wants me and nobody loves me—but here is someone who seems genuinely interested in me as a person. They want to learn about my life, and are disproportionately interested in everything that has happened to me. What is more, nothing I say, however unflattering or unseemly, makes them think any less of me.

All this takes time, as I have been reminded over and over again at Mill Grove. Why should a child trust me enough to share anything of importance with me until I have demonstrated that I am wholly worthy of such trust? But the patience that is willing to wait is equally important in showing the significance of that child as a person.[15]

The relationship of unconditional commitment, like security and boundaries, must be internalized, because no one can guarantee that a particular person will always be physically present. One of the important stages in a relationship comes when people are separated. Does each person carry the other with them in their mind? This is a crucial matter for very young children. If they begin to sense that their parent forgets them—not in the sense of not knowing their name, but because other people and problems tend to drive them out of the parent's mind—it is deeply unsettling. It can lead to attention-seeking and will always engender anxiety. At the other end of the spectrum is the parent who always holds the child in his or her thoughts wherever the child happens to be, thinking of the child at nursery and at night, and imagining the world through the child's eyes. This makes for healthy internalization of the other person.[16]

AFFIRMATION OF SKILLS AND CREATIONS

It is important for the growing child to know that what he or she makes, paints, achieves or does is valued by another consistent adult.

Let me be clear: 'value' here does not mean that the child's creation changes or 'buys' the relationship. The real significance of a person lies not in what they do or make, but in the fact that they are valued in themselves and without conditions. So whatever the child makes, it is not done or presented to prove that the child should be favoured. The child may see it in this way, and may seek approval for this reason, but that is not what the process should be about. I am talking about noticing what the child says and does, makes and shapes, and affirming the effort. In some way, everything that we make is part of us, so the way people respond to these things indicates how they feel about us.

This affirmation starts with noticing when the child points at things, being guided by this pointing, and describing what you see. Then, when the child can pick up and carry things, affirmation consists in receiving them from the child. Then comes the time when something is painted, sung, created. In each and every case it is important that parents respond positively and, in my view, honestly. It is always possible to speak the truth with grace. We should not give the impression that every child is a budding Cezanne or Bach, but we can admire aspects of what they have created; we can and must encourage their endeavours. (We will return to this in Chapter Seven.) One of my abiding childhood memories is the way my father used to make time to watch me play football and cricket for my school teams. He also helped me practise both sports. In turn, I did the same thing with my son. It is a simple but telling way of affirming the significance of a child.

As I have mentioned, my friend and colleague Dr Jo-Joy Wright has begun to develop the five themes of this book in her own clinical work with children and teaching. She uses the term 'responsivity' for what I have been describing here. This implies that a parent figure is available, that he or she is in some ways in tune with the child emotionally, and that this tunefulness will enable appropriate responses, reactions and, where necessary, interventions. It is critical for children to know that they are 'being heard'—that there is an active witness of their actions and feelings.

At the appropriate time, one of the most constructive things that a parent can do is to provide a child with opportunities to undertake errands and tasks, and thus to experience what it is like to become a valued member of a community who is able to contribute to the common good. When a child makes a practical contribution, it changes the dynamics of a relationship that started with the adult providing the most help and support. To avoid creating a dependency relationship, the child must be allowed opportunities to reciprocate that help and support in some way, however small. I wonder whether the malaise among so many teenagers in the affluent West has anything to do with the decline in opportunities to help their families or communities in practical ways.

Just as one of the chief privileges for a Christian is to be a partner with God in his mission of caring for creation and reconciling the whole of the cosmos to himself, so a great privilege for a child is to be invited to cooperate in the tasks of daily life—to be accepted as worthy of responsibility. Being entrusted with tasks encourages the agency of the child rather than dependency and passivity. It helps create a sense of focused and planned activity, which has an important purpose in the process of taking responsibility and appropriate control over aspects of his or her personal life.

Helping can be great fun. One of the games that my grandson likes playing most with me is fetching the paper and milk from the doorstep and putting the milk in the fridge. Only yesterday he helped with the rinsing at Mill Grove after the evening meal. There were 20 or so people present, so there was quite a lot to do, but at the end he was disappointed that there was no more.

I AND THOU

Like many, I am so grateful for Martin Buber's seminal work *I and Thou*.[17] It has sat among my favourite books since I first read it over

20 years ago. Buber divides relationships into two basic types: 'I/it' and 'I/thou'. In the former, the relationship is like that between a scientist and the materials being studied, a cook and a cake, a builder and bricks, a farmer and livestock and so on. The latter relationship is possible only between two human beings or between humans and God.

In the 'I/it' relationship, the subject is always the 'I', and the 'I' acts on the 'it'. In the 'I/thou' relationship, both the 'I' and the 'thou' are potential subjects. This relationship is therefore reciprocal, with the way each sees the other affecting the development of the relationship. My view of 'thou' acts on your view of me, and vice versa. It is about being equals, but about the quality of commitment, understanding and respect between the two. Obviously, when a child is part of such a relationship, he or she will tend to take on board his own significance.

Much that is written about children, child-rearing and teaching ultimately depends on the notion that there is a group of adults who are in control and who decide how to act on the child or children, with a given set of expectations or 'learning outcomes'. But where is there room in all this for the 'thou' of the child? Children are human beings, deserving of respect and recognition for their being and agency, not just in the future 'when they have been educated' but in the here and now. What they think, feel, fear and desire matters and should be taken into the reckoning.

The agency and integrity of children should be taken seriously in any learning situation for children—school, home or church—and this is why I have such respect for the Godly Play system of religious learning or play. Adults have responsibility for creating the setting in which the encounter takes place and for telling the story, but children are active participants in the process. The crucial reflections at the end are not questions but musings: 'I wonder what part of the story you liked best', for example. Children make important decisions about what to say, when to keep silent, how to pray and so on. Godly Play sessions are typified by the 'I/thou' relationship, whereas much of what goes on in church and Sunday school, as in so many institutions, is based more closely on the 'I/it' relationship.

BIBLICAL INSIGHTS

Before looking at some of the biblical insights into this theme, I would like to share something that continues to surface in my writings and thinking. I wonder whether it is possible for a child to develop a sense of meaning and significance without a religious dimension to the world of their childhood. By this I do not mean an acquaintance with one or more religions but an experience of religion incorporated into their whole interpretation of events, rituals and feelings. In the light of Richard Dawkins' writing on the 'God delusion' and the way he sees religion abusing children, it may be helpful to quote Erik Erikson: 'The clinician can only observe that many are proud to be without religion whose children cannot afford their being without it. On the other hand there are many who seem to derive a vital faith from social action or scientific action or scientific pursuit.'[18]

However attractive it may sound to say that children will find out for themselves what they believe, children do need to develop a sense that those around them believe in something that gives meaning to life.[19] I am not sure that we have given sufficient attention to this matter in considering the nature of childhood. That being said, the Bible assumes a religious framework and describes ways in which a child can be surrounded by a family, community and society that nurture significance.

With this theme, we come to something very close to the heart of the biblical narrative and of God's nature. As we acknowledged in Chapter Three, death and nothingness threaten every human being with the fear that their lives are of no ultimate significance. 'Is there any meaning to be found in my life?' is an anxiety in every person and every era. 'Nothing makes sense!' observes the writer of the biblical book of Ecclesiastes (1:2), and this is indeed one eminently reasonable view of history. The Bible allows this view plenty of space for development, yet at the core of the unfolding story is a God who values each person infinitely. This is the biblical account in the face of everything that seems to suggest that the human race in general, and the life of a child in particular, are of little or no significance.

The Bible presents the idea that people are of infinite value in a variety of ways—through events, stories and the oracles of prophets. One theme is that all humans, not just Jesus, are made in the image of God (see Genesis 1:27). If we are looking for an image of God, it is provided in each little child: we do not have to create or search for other representations of God. Recently I had the privilege of listening to an antique dealer telling me about his impressions after he had read through the whole Bible for the very first time. He had not come from a Christian family, so he was starting from scratch. He commented that one of the most consistent messages of the Bible was that God treated idolatry very seriously—and that indeed is an underrated thread of the Bible narrative. The reason for it is important: God has already given us images of himself in human beings. Thus every alternative representation is, in effect, a rejection of God's chosen image. Idols demean human beings, and idol worship will lead, over time, to humans debasing themselves.

So all of us human beings, whatever our age, abilities or disabilities, are of ultimate significance because we are made in God's image. We are signs or symbols of God himself. Whatever our relationship to the rest of the planet and to the natural world, including other animate species, humans are unique in the Bible in this respect. A child will therefore discover in the Bible how very significant he or she is to God.

There are many who see in theologies of children a 'poisonous pedagogy', on account of the way the wilfulness and sinfulness of children is emphasized.[20] In the biblical narrative, however, sin is not the starting point for an understanding of children: the creation of human beings in the image of God predates sin. There is paradise, and paradise lost, not only in the biblical record but also in the psychic life of each child.[21]

The story of redemption that runs throughout the Bible must be seen in this context. As a result of human rebellion, pride and wilfulness, there is disruption of the relationship between humans and God, and also of human relationships with fellow human beings and the rest of creation. The Bible describes how God intervened to reestablish this relationship and negate the effects of sin. Stories and covenants describe how greatly God loves his people, and the lengths to which he will go in order to reconcile them to himself.

The message is that although God demands obedience to the laws and covenant he has established, his love is not dependent on our good living. The people of Israel are characterized by Moses as obstinate and prone to rebel against God (although they had their times of obedience), but God is gracious to them and his steadfast love endures for ever.

Many Bible stories focus on the community of God, but there is also evidence that God will do anything to win back a single human being to himself. Jesus' stories of the father of two sons, who welcomes the lost one back as his own beloved child (the 'prodigal' son in Luke 15:11–24), and the shepherd who loses a single sheep and goes out to search for it until he finds it (15:4–6), are about God's love for a single person. The message seems to be that God will go to any length to save that single person.

God is unconditionally committed to each human being: that is how much we matter to him. Not only do Christians believe that the universe as a whole is significant to God; they also believe that each and every person is significant. The early part of the Old Testament is about the God of Abraham, Isaac and Jacob. In each story there are detailed descriptions of the encounters between a

God who cares deeply for individuals and their families, and establishes 'covenants' with them, and particular named individuals who wrestle with the enormity of this reality.

Wherever we find descriptions of this God intervening in the lives of adult individuals (and these recur throughout the Bible), the most common reaction of the person concerned is a feeling of wonder, awe and unworthiness. They simply cannot conceive that they should be of such value or significance to God. They feel unworthy of his attention, his promises and the responsibilities with which he entrusts them. By contrast, when the individual is a child, there is a different response: whether or not they understand the significance of what is going on, we do not always know, but they do not immediately feel unworthy. They tend to accept the love and responsibility being offered to them. We can see this in the stories of Joseph, Samuel, David and, later, Jesus as a boy, as well as in the children who responded to Jesus' voice, call and touch.

However mixed the messages a child receives about his or her worth from other human beings, the biblical story is one in which he or she is of such significance that God will go to extraordinary lengths to demonstrate his steadfast love. Many millions of children live and die without receiving from other human beings any assurance of their self-worth and value, but in such cases, where children are despised and rejected, Jesus teaches that their guardian angels 'continually see the face' of his Father in heaven (Matthew 18:10, NRSV). Whatever this may mean, it communicates the love and commitment at the heart of God for every person.

We saw in Chapter Three that our many different understandings of the death of Jesus all boil down to an irreducible core that is about an inner security, not just a safe physical space. This security has been created because we are so significant to God that in Jesus he was willing to assume not only our humanity but also our sin and rebellion, in order that we might be restored to a relationship of love with him.

I recall, as a boy, hearing more than one preacher suggest that we ought to put our own names into John 3:16 ('God loved [Keith] so much...') in order to see something of the magnitude of God's love for us personally. The great hymn writers like Charles Wesley try to express this magnitude—'Amazing love, how can it be that thou, my God, should'st die for me?'—but it is impossible to grasp the extent of our significance to God.

The Pavement Project is a resource pioneered by my colleague and friend, Gundelina Velazco, from the Philippines. She and her team get alongside street children in different parts of the world and seek to empathize with their experiences and stories. By careful use of pictures and the stories of Jesus, they link the feelings of each child with the stories of Jesus about God's love for them. The effects have been really remarkable: every child responds in some way to this great truth. They may be insignificant to their families, peers and other human beings, but in the sight of God they matter as much as the one lost sheep to the shepherd who leaves everything to find it.

The whole of the biblical story, Christian worship and Christian life revolve around this unfathomable revelation of God's love for us. When human beings commit themselves unconditionally to another person, they are therefore reflecting in some way this love at the heart of things. That is what Paul says of the marriage relationship: it is a sign of God's love for his people and his covenant with them (Ephesians 5:25–33). This love draws and inspires each Christian but it is also a model for our lives. When two individuals come to believe that nothing can ever come between them and that their love is for eternity, the band of gold and the diamond in the engagement ring are symbols of their 'undying' love. Somewhere in this process, there must be a sense of the significance of oneself, in order to understand the significance of the other and to trust the other in their inexplicable lavishing of love on oneself. This insight into significance is a prerequisite of the growth of love.

The very idea of such love (imperfect as it may be in practice) is based on a fundamental understanding of the significance and worth of the self. This understanding does not grow out of thin air, but reflects the unconditional commitment of another person in early life. Therefore, it is important that the growing child sees lived examples of sustained and committed relationships involving affection, in a world increasingly dominated by media portrayals of sexual connections and short-term encounters.

We are often told that our unconditional commitment to children at Mill Grove is remarkable. My own feeling is that it shouldn't be remarkable for a follower of Jesus to offer such commitment. This is surely the example that Jesus set and the message he taught. In response to God's love, what sacrifice or commitment can a human being make that is too great, too lavish? Paul calls on us all, in view of God's love, to 'offer [our] bodies to him as a living sacrifice' (Romans 12:1). The language is stunning. So, in calling for unconditional commitment to other human beings, I am simply restating what I believe to be at the core of the gospel. I can see how professionals and unions would question such a calling, but I do not see that Christians have any option about it.

If this message were to become reality in the lives of Christians around the world, it would transform the lives of children who, at present, lack anyone to stand alongside them and to treat them as their own.

SUMMARY

There is much that combines to undermine the growing child's sense of meaning and significance, yet the biblical revelation is that each child is of priceless worth and significance to God. There are many ways in which this sense of significance can be nurtured and affirmed, but a key is the unconditional commitment of at least one adult throughout childhood. This 'now' of unconditional love ultimately derives from and mirrors God's unconditional commitment, and helps to pave the way for the 'not yet', when the child will be able to give and receive love in new ways and with more self-consciousness.

Chapter Six

COMMUNITY

Very old people with walking sticks will once again sit around in Jerusalem, while boys and girls play in the streets.

Zechariah 8:4–5

BEYOND FAMILY AND HOME

The little child starts in a womb and a family. The family constitutes his or her world, but we adults know that this is only a tiny fragment of the wider social world to which the child will be introduced in time. It is widely accepted that children have a built-in capacity and desire for relationships with others beyond their siblings and parents (the 'outside world').[1] From an early age, young children find ways of relating to peers without recourse to language and by using simple forms of play. I cannot stress too much the importance of play in the growth of love, in this case by facilitating appropriate social interaction.

Families are mediators in the process of engagement. They 'contain' the child at the outset and later represent the wider world. The time comes when they encourage the young person to make his or her own way in the world. There are many predictable potential risks to the growth of love along the way, and there are many potential joys and blessings. All who are 'parents' (villagers), whether in family or community, will want to strike a balance between security and exploration, 'us' and 'them', safety and risk, adult traditions and the new insights of children in a rapidly changing global context. The question is not if children need community; it is how best to facilitate their proper participation in the social and civic life. Here we reflect on the contribution of 'communities' to the growth of love.

We will be considering the web or network of relationships and the many-layered connections of the public space sometimes labelled 'civil society'. Both family and state depend on this rich tapestry of social groups and processes for their nurture and well-being. If love is to grow within and beyond families, then this realm, which we might well think of as the social compost of the child and family's life, is vital for the functioning and well-being of the family.

It can be a revealing exercise to chart one's own life story using the categories of family, peer groups, schools, mass media, neighbourhood, church, clubs and friends, because it reveals how much of a social creature a human being is. It calls into question what we mean by 'individual', which is, in some respects, an abstract concept or ideal type. Individuals derive from relationships, develop within them, depend on them and normally long for them. Yet one of the words often used in books on socialization and in policies for looked-after children is 'independence'. Those who are caring for children in the UK are supposed to be 'preparing them for independence'. Because this is palpably less than the whole truth, I always rewrite the word as 'interdependence'. Social life is the context, stuff and daily reality of human development and identity.

We must note, however, that the experience of belonging is about mutual relationships, but also exclusion. Communities are possible only where there are boundaries: this is 'our community' and that is 'not our community'—it is 'beyond the pale', comprised of 'outsiders'. Community is, like everything else on earth, double-edged. It can be a source of support, affirmation and learning while at the same time being divisive, threatening and inward-looking.

ELECTRONIC COMMUNICATION

Before looking at how children engage with those outside their immediate families, we pause to take in the huge and increasing impact of electronic media on the lives of children. This may well be one of the most important factors in current and future understandings of childhood. The internet will have an impact beyond our imagining on the social world of the next and subsequent generations. Whatever its benefits, it also opens the way for children and young people to be exploited by media and groups without the awareness—and therefore without the protection and mediation—of their families.

The desire to belong lies at the heart of much advertising directed at children and young people. The mega media corporations are now close to providing, for some children, a complete pattern, routine and canopy for their social life, including film, CDs, merchandise and magazines. Thus peer groups are guided toward topics for discussion, commodities to desire and games to play—until, that is, the next new film is released and the whole little universe is recreated.

The early signs are that many children have already retreated into their own rooms, curtains often drawn, as they connect to virtual groups, clubs, chatrooms and communities. One effect of this development is on the fabric of the daily life of families. When we use the term 'family life', I wonder whether we have caught up with the huge changes in actual living patterns, family contact and the organization of space, relationships and authority in households that has taken place in the past 40 years.

Television depends on the notion of virtual communities. Football clubs are, for most supporters worldwide, actually virtual communities, and the club shirts are very important in the sense of belonging and meaning that they give to young people. This is identity not as something that is distinctive and uniquely 'me', but identity in its deeper and original meaning of 'that which I have in common with others'.

FAMILY AND COMMUNITY

Although there is no necessary and universal process by which all children go through identifiable and discrete stages of development and growth, we noted in Chapter Two that there is an inherent or implicit progression. It is likely that a positive experience of community cannot precede the establishment of security and significance. Likewise, it is necessary to understand some of the basics of boundaries before being able to understand, cope with and enjoy social intercourse.[2]

On the other hand, community is an ever-present reality, of which child and family are a part, and a child's sense of security, boundaries and significance derive in no small part from this community. This is not to suggest, however, that there is a neat progression, as if community can be entered and experienced only after, as it were, passing exams in the other three subjects: security, boundaries and significance.

The child's family and language will normally be two of the primary ways into wider communities. Or, to put it the other way round, the family will be a means by which communities find their way into the being and soul of a child. How does this happen? Largely by means of rituals—that is, repeated events or routines. Rituals are vital to every social group, and are the primary means by which children are initiated into those groups.[3]

Let me give a simple personal example. How did Tottenham Hotspur football club become part of me and I of it? It was through my family. When I was a very little boy, every Saturday we would gather in my grandparents' front room and grandpa would put the radio on for *Sports Report*. I can still hum the theme tune perfectly without even thinking about it. The announcer would begin with the results of Football League Division One, and it wasn't long before I picked up the fact that one team was far more important than any other.

The whole room accepted grandpa's allegiance to a team founded in 1882 by a teacher in a Bible class at All Hallows Church, Tottenham. When I could read newspapers, I naturally looked for the results of Spurs before any other, and when I was old enough to go to a match, guess who we watched?

This is a simple example of how a family can mediate between the child and the wider social world. For Tottenham Hotspur, read clubs, groups, parties, faith communities and so on. In time young people have to decide for themselves whether to accept all these identifications and associations or not, but at the outset the child knows nothing else: this is the way things are. Children need help to negotiate this complex and potentially confusing contradictory world beyond the household. Electronic media may well supplant parents in much of this process: it is too early to draw conclusions.

Understanding the world of nature, with its pattern of day and night, seasons, trees, wind and breeze, movement of animals and plants, water, fire, ice, earth and so on, is an adventure and challenge of significant proportions that needs interpretation—but so does the world of social relationships. I think of the child arriving on his or her mother's back at a bazaar in a village in India.[4] There is a bewildering array and confused interaction of sensations, including scents, sounds, colours and movements. How on earth can the child make any sense of this community? One of the answers, of course, is by repetition. Tuesday by Tuesday, the child will come back, and gradually patterns will emerge.

The parent of the child is part of this community, so the family is like a bridge or go-between, linking the child to the community. Perhaps, in our quest for individual growth, fulfilment, agency and rights, we have been in danger of overlooking the way in which families are little communities. In faith communities, families are little churches, temples, mosques or synagogues. We tend to distinguish between the family and the outside world, but I would argue that this conceptualization is, at best, only part of the truth.

Communities are modelled for the growing child in and by families. Bear in mind that, as we saw at the end of Chapter Two

('Stooping to enter the world of childhood'), the family is the child's whole world. It is within the family that the child learns about mealtimes, conversations, visits, housework, play, the organization of the house, beds, tables, chairs, kitchen utensils, food and food preparation, television and household goods—but the way the family experiences these things will reflect assumptions and traditions in the wider community. So family is the instrument by which a child learns about how the community lives, what it values, how it organizes time, space, conversation, conflict, distribution of wealth and so on.

There are two main reasons why I see this insight as significant. First, it helps in understanding how family and church (faith community) should relate to each other (and we will come back to this). Second, it shows that if the family is traumatized, broken, disrupted and therefore dysfunctional, children will find themselves separated from the wider community in addition to whatever problems they encounter in their own being and in close relationships with parents and siblings. We may have underestimated the potentially severe effects of this disruption and social isolation.[5]

SCHOOLS

Increasingly, the nations of the world agree that it is desirable for all children to go to school. That is one of the rights set out in the 1989 UN Convention on the Rights of the Child.[6] If this means that all children should have the right to appropriate learning, training and education, who could disagree? But if it means that all children must be placed in rooms with 30 or so other children five days a week, then it will not do.

Many children seem reasonably happy with some sort of arrangement whereby they learn along with others. There is much evidence of sensitivity in the preparation of children for a new school, in forging helpful links with parents and families, and in the awareness of children's personal and social functioning. However, a fundamental overhaul of what we mean by 'education' worldwide is overdue. The impetus for this overhaul is coming from several quarters. There is an acknowledgment that current systems have much in common with industrialization and production lines (historically, universal schooling for children often arrived in a society at about the same time as urban factories); there is a growing awareness that children have not been seen as agents in the process of learning or constructing the learning environment; there is the mushrooming of electronic communication, which may leave many aspects of traditional education redundant; there is a sense that schools should be moral communities and address emotional intelligence; and there is, of course, the need to work out how attachment theory and the substance of this book may be incorporated into the learning process.

Like families, schools mediate between the growing child and the wider world of economics, politics, religion and society. Also, like families, they are not just functional bridges: they actually embody values and assumptions. If love is to grow, then schools need to be sensitive to the process and their part in it. I am increasingly concerned about the number of children who seem to be failed by the existing systems in this respect.

In my experience, many children find conventional schooling inappropriate. Where there is no attachment or bonding, there will be little sense of self, so a child may be threatened psychologically to the point of fear of annihilation by being put in a group of other children. This may manifest itself in a range of ways, including the desire to control situations, disrupt a class, to be expelled and so on.

Speaking as one who had a generally happy and even fulfilling school career, my experience and reading of the situation lead me to question the extent of the difficulties inherent in the social dynamics of much schooling, by which I mean the assumptions woven into the way we do education. Given the unknown implications of the internet on our whole way of communicating, relating, accessing information and learning, I wonder how historians will see our school buildings in, say, 100 years' time. It is not fanciful to imagine that many of them, like former workhouses, ragged schools and psychiatric hospitals, will be museums. (This is not to question the creativity, professionalism and commitment of many teachers, boards of governors and school communities, but rather to set the issue in a much broader historical context.)

With so many children identified as having certain syndromes and prescribed with Ritalin and related drugs to help them maintain a 'normal life', has it occurred to our society that we might openly discuss whether the treatment should be of the pupils or the social and cultural world of which they are a part? I suspect that there is a fundamental problem here, which, like the prevalence of bullying in schools, we are reluctant to explore.

Because schools are so important in the lives of growing children, it is vital that they are carefully reassessed in the light of what we know about the growth of love.

CHURCH AS COMMUNITY

For children who are part of Christian families, the local church functions as a community in its own right, with its own meetings, rituals and beliefs. It is also representative of wider communities, linking the growing child to other people and families beside kin, to the nation through prayers and events like Remembrance Sunday, and to the world through its worldwide connections and members.

Churches have many roles and functions, but one that may be underestimated is that of a mediator between the child, the family and the wider community. I am not sure whether many churches would identify this as a role of any importance beside more conventional descriptions of children's ministry. In the conventional model, the church provides particular space for children and child-related activities, including religious teaching, but does not necessarily see itself as a living community in which children play their part in the life of the whole, and through which they are equipped and motivated to help and serve local communities. Where this mediating role is taken seriously, however, there are several implications.

First, churches will not routinely choose to split the family by age, so that its members find themselves separated for much of the worship and other activities. Rather, churches will want to model a variety of relationships in society, which might include family, clubs, teams, associations, communities of scholars, assemblies, parliaments and informal friendships. There will be shared meals, shared worship, shared learning, shared decision-making, shared helping in the community and shared engagement in global mission. Sunday schools, in this way of thinking, will explicitly acknowledge that everyone is a learner whatever their age, and will not necessarily mirror what goes on in schools. All-age worship, likewise, will accept children as a natural and integral part of the whole worshipping community of faith, and it will not always be the children and young people for whom 'it is now time to go to your own activities'.

Second, as argued in Chapter Four, churches will choose to take very seriously the Ten Commandments, which specifically relate the growing child to the social world. The commandments will be taught to children, not as a distinct group within a segmented church but sometimes as part of biological families, sometimes as part of the whole church family. I commend using the command-ments in inclusive church worship, so that they can be articulated by everyone.

Third, churches will choose to see families as 'little churches', trying to serve families instead of seeking to draw families into church. It will be seen as a two-way, dynamic process—a reciprocal relationship in which the church sees one of its priorities as helping the parents to be good ministers of the gospel to their children in the whole of life, including the daily sacraments of meals, prayers and work, and by word and example. We have underestimated how much true worship occurs around the meal table, on holidays, at bedtimes and at all times in between.

Fourth, churches will choose to take upon themselves a conscious role of training children for citizenship in local communities, cities, nations and the world. When I was a boy, I was part of a missionary movement called Ropeholders. It was the junior section of the Baptist Missionary Society. My parents were members of Christian Endeavour. Membership was age-related and it was taken for granted that we would remain members until we reached the next stage. In such groups, our generations experienced and learned something of what it meant to play an active role in mission, to think beyond ourselves and beyond our church and localities. The focus was not on self-fulfilment, entertainment or even spiritual development so much as the service of others. I am not sure what the modern-day equivalent of these groups might be.

Fifth, churches will set less store by how they function as institutions or organizations (numbers and success, vision and so on), and more by the quality of relationships within and between families. A church bursting with activities may undervalue the ordinary family life of its members. There is the need for a careful balance between the activities that a church organizes for its members (and others) and the space it allows for families within it to pursue their own agendas, whether in daily life and work or with regard to holidays and festivals. It cannot be assumed that a well-functioning church will manifest its good health by the range and number of events and activities for which it is responsible. In promoting this balance, it is vital to consider all types of family, including those that are struggling and feel incomplete.

In general, I agree with my late friend Bruce Reed, who felt that the Jewish community had got the relationship between assembly and families working far better than most churches. The synagogue is important as a focal point but it does not supplant or detract from the family, seeking rather to serve and enhance family life.

THE WIDER WORLD

Much of what is meant by and experienced as 'security' has to do with something like a 'homeland'—roots, and a sense of belonging. For some people, this 'homeland' may be primarily their family, typified by the importance attached to their family tree. For others, it may be politics, a cause, a religious faith or a sense of belonging to a nation or 'race'.[7] In time, children begin to identify with groups and causes beyond kith and kin, and the internet means that connections can be made, for an increasing number, on a global scale.

In cases where family, neighbourhood and society do not protect and affirm an individual directly or indirectly, a person may turn to a radical cause, like a liberation movement, for community.[8] I would contend that all of us, as children, instinctively seek to attach ourselves to at least one other person on earth who is totally committed to us. If we find that person or persons, we will have identified at least part of what belonging is about. Other relationships will tend to complement and supplement this primary attachment. However, if we have not established a good enough attachment to an individual or family-type group, consciously or unconsciously we will still be seeking this primal sense of belonging.

One of the recurring tragedies of history is that leaders of groups and organizations exploit their followers' insecurity for their own purposes. Hitler, for example, who may well have lacked satisfactory attachment himself as a child, appealed with huge success to two concepts: 'volk'[9] and motherland. Both provided fundamental community and a sense of solidarity within a wider group, and children were seen as integral to his whole political strategy.

We do well to ask what this analysis has to do with current Islamic radicalism among young people living in the West. Are they living in a liminal zone of ambivalence, where they do not feel they belong? If so, they may be drawn to something that offers them an ultimate cause or sense of belonging: a band of brothers. Perhaps their alienation represents a more intense version of what everyone is feeling as globalization gathers apace.

BIBLICAL INSIGHTS INTO COMMUNITY

Once again, as we turn to the scriptures we find a rich vein of insights into community.

Beyond individuals

We start with the observation that although the Bible describes the lives of individuals and many and varied encounters between individuals and God, it sets these stories within the unfolding narrative of the formation, life, struggles and rebirth of communities. The culmination of the prophetic message in both the Old and New Testaments (see Isaiah and Revelation) focuses on the creation of new communities where people of all ages, stages, cultures and conditions dwell together in peace and harmony. Individuals are not lost in this new community; they are called to play their part and find fulfilment in communities of faith. So there is a wealth of material to draw on as we consider the nature of community in the lives of growing children and young people.

The many biblical metaphors for this life together stress not uniformity but the interdependence of different parts. One of the pictures that the apostle Paul delights in is his portrayal of the Church as a body, with Christ as its head and the members as different parts of the body. There is organic unity and mutual service and feeling, but the parts have not ceased to be different. In his first letter to the believers in Corinth (1 Corinthians 12:12–30), Paul challenges the idea of uniformity by imagining what the body would look like if it were all ear or eye (v. 17).

It is possible that history will identify our contemporary era as a period in which the rise of individual consumerism and human rights became socially unsustainable. If so, it is our children and their children who will need to find new ways (we cannot go back) to balance and integrate individual freedom and rights with social relationships and responsibilities in recreated communities. In such a process, they will find the biblical narrative and theological reflections in both the Old and New Testaments to be a great resource.

Covenant as the basis of family and community

In exploring the interface between families and community in the life of a child, we must be careful not to make the mistake of seeing families, however socially significant they may be, as the 'basic building blocks of societies'. For a start, societies are not like buildings—they are far more organic—but there is a far more important reason: it is 'covenant' that is vital for the survival of all social groups, including families. If we take the most basic of groups—the dyad between a male and a female—the Bible sets it within the covenant of marriage. This may seem like splitting hairs, but it is of fundamental importance. Legally, cohabitation has little if anything in common with marriage, and if we are to understand what the Bible has to teach about the growth of love, we do well to reframe our understanding of the meaning of love in the light of the importance of covenant.

The basis of the relations between God and his people, founded on and emanating in love, is covenant. We read of the covenants between God and Abraham, Isaac, Jacob, and then with his chosen people through Moses. In the New Testament, there is a new covenant sealed with the blood of Jesus. Love is made possible through covenants, and this causes us to consider what we mean by 'love'. It is certainly not about temporary feelings and emotions, but enduring and steadfast commitment. Paul's description in 1 Corinthians 13 is probably one of the best expositions: love never gives up (vv. 7–8).

Marriage makes a huge difference in the lives of children: it is something firm that they can understand, and this covenant is the biblical basis for family life. There has been a bold if not reckless experiment going on in the West since the 1960s with cohabitation —that is, adults living together with no form of public commitment. It will be several generations before we see what effect this has had on the lives of children and the nature of family and community life, but to assume that love can thrive in a climate where covenant is not the norm is to make a huge leap of faith.[10]

In practice, I believe it is vital for children, from a very young age, to be present at events and ceremonies where the solemn and binding nature of covenants is expressed. Such an occasion occurred when Ezra was reading aloud from the scroll in Jerusalem (Nehemiah 8:1–18), and every child old enough to understand what was being read would have sensed that something extraordinary was going on. It was the discovery of the covenant that had been allowed to lapse.

I have watched very small children at weddings and baptisms, on Remembrance Sunday, at funerals and at services of rededication and commitment, such as the Methodist Covenant service or a Boys' or Girls' Brigade leaders' act of commitment. At first I was surprised by what I observed: the younger the children, the more they seemed to be engaged by the ceremony. Children thrive in the social space created when adults engage in special activities where children are present but not the objects of the activity.[11] I wonder whether this type of 'space' is particularly fertile ground in which the seeds of love take root and grow. One of my concerns is that families—like schools, churches and clubs—have tended to undervalue such occasions and even to exclude children from them (think of Holy Communion and funerals). We can do better for our children.

I recently attended a very special wedding in Banbury, Oxfordshire. I sat beside some young children during the service and wondered where on earth in their lives they would encounter such a beautiful representation of covenant in which a whole community was fully engaged. Then it dawned on me that many children will never be part of a service like this. That being so, where will they experience the real-life drama of marriage affirmed by families and the community of which they are a part?

Institutions such as monarchy

Given that a child's family seems like a little kingdom, it should not be surprising that kings and queens are archetypes that he or she instinctively understands. Fairy stories and pantomime plots remind children that, in families, Mum and Dad are the rulers of the realm (with variations on the theme). Whether children grow up in monarchies or republics, there must be respect for the rule of law balanced against the right to stand up for conscience and against tyranny, deceit and totalitarian oppression.

Worldwide, throughout history, children have both benefited from and suffered at the hands of governments of every kind. The scriptures are ambivalent about political states, particularly the monarchy. States often oppress people and not infrequently depend on some form of slavery, and the establishment of the monarchy in Israel was incongruent with the belief that God was Israel's ruler. The story of the monarchy as given in the two books of Kings is a salutary one indeed, and in the New Testament Jesus and his followers are constantly living in tension with the national institutions as well as the Roman rulers.

Family and church need to teach and model ways of operating and making decisions with reference to the prevailing government. Childhood is a time when enquiry into such things is natural. When our youngest child was growing up in the UK, our monarch was Queen Elizabeth II and our Prime Minister was Mrs Margaret Thatcher. This confused our daughter, who concluded that the real queen was Mrs Thatcher because, although she did not wear a crown, she certainly had all the power. We might tend to praise our own child for such political insight, but it could be wiser to conclude that children generally are able to digest more information about a national government than adults assume. Perhaps the filtering of the biblical narrative in Sunday schools and children's Bibles has tended to neglect this whole area.

While working on this book, I have also been writing various pieces on Child Theology. This has presented me with some challenges about what to include in each of my writings. Because another book and papers include much on the kingdom of heaven,[12] I have decided to deal lightly with the subject here, but this chapter would be incomplete and even invalid were it to be omitted altogether. There is a synergy between children and the kingdom of heaven that merits deep reflection. This kingdom is primarily about neither the virtues and spirituality of individuals nor the structure of groups (whether churches or states). I prefer to describe it as 'God's way of living' or 'where God has his way'. You can test out the definition by reading the parables in Matthew's Gospel using this paraphrase: 'God's way of doing things is like what happens when a farmer plants a mustard seed… [or] when a woman mixes a little yeast into three big batches of flour' (13:31, 33).

Perhaps this is the place to clarify how the different Gospel writers describe this kingdom. John does not refer to it as such, but Luke and Mark both call it 'the kingdom of God'. Matthew, reluctant to use the holy word 'God' where he can avoid it, prefers the term 'kingdom of heaven' (literally 'kingdom of the heavens or skies'). In all cases, the dynamic equivalent 'where God has his way' is appropriate.

This kingdom—which is not to be confused with a place, an order, a hierarchy, church or any other institution—represents the breaking into human life and relationships of a new set of values and priorities. These values were lived out and modelled supremely by Jesus Christ in his relationships with his special followers as well as the other people he met. The early believers in Jerusalem lived in a distinctively radical way (see Acts 2:42–47; 4:32–37), and it remains a matter of debate how far this model is normative for church today.

I do not see children as being particularly virtuous or evil: they seem to me to be a mixture of both in the same measure as in adults. However, because they are young, enquiring, learning, testing, moving and challenging, they can facilitate the dynamics of new ways of living. They can lead, not in the sense of teaching adults in a formal way but by their questions and challenges. While valuing the security of familiar rituals and patterns of life, they are also inherently adaptable, changing and flexible.

In case we have not made the obvious link, the kingdom of heaven is not about control, ownership, possessions, wealth and fame, but about love. We might say that it reflects the sunlight of God's love and nurtures the growth of love in humans. Such love is not a sentimental, self-obsessed, romantic or sexual love, detached from the rest of social life; it is a love that relates to every part of the social world. It is strong love, if it needs to be, resisting tyranny and oppression, but it is gentle love, too, where the little child is feeling bullied, ignored or undervalued. Christians are led by Jesus Christ to see and interpret every aspect of life, from family to state, through the radical lens offered by this kingdom.

When adults give their lives to live alongside children and are committed to them (mothers most usually, but also people like Janusz Korczak), the quality of their relationships becomes increasingly like those lived by Jesus. It is as if, by welcoming children, the kingdom itself is realized: the king has been received. No amount of psychological, spiritual or political thought or engineering will usher in this kingdom, but in accepting little children a change takes place. Career, instrumentality, domination and so on begin to recede and take a back seat: what really matters is quite different from what drives the earthly rulers and authorities.

If we leave children out of our philosophical, political and theological discourses, I do not see how we will ever glimpse in practice what the kingdom of God is all about. In this kingdom, love is given and received with no account of merit, desert or rank.

Jesus and community

I hope it is already clear that if we are looking for insights into the nature and working of community, Jesus will be one of our very best guides. The Gospels portray him as one who is deeply interested in the personal stories and lives of those who come to him or have chosen to live alongside him; aware of the very real challenges of political life and authority; sensitive to ethnic tensions, cultures and traditions. But he is described as plotting a new course through all of this—a way of living together that has room for the social outcasts as well as the leaders, for men and women, and for children.

So often, Jesus' life is talked, preached and written about as if it were the life of an individual relating to other individuals. That is a precious part of the story, but Jesus also establishes a new community. Children are not only part of that life together; they are vital clues to how God would have the community live.

As we ponder each of these aspects and levels of community with children in mind, I hope we will find new insights and perspectives that help us to explore scripture and daily living in fresh ways. It takes a big leap to go against the spirit and assumptions of our own time, and this is what the theme of community may require us to do. If you reread the Gospels while bearing in mind the child, Jesus, the kingdom of heaven and community, you will find, if my experience is anything to go by, a gentle revolution taking place. We are not thinking simply of how communities facilitate the growth of love in children, but how children facilitate the growth of love in communities.

Pentecost

As we continue to explore the theme of community in the Bible with children in mind, it would be strange to overlook Pentecost. The day of Pentecost, when the gift of the Holy Spirit was poured out on the disciples in Jerusalem (Acts 2:1–4), can be seen as a counterpoint to the overweening concentration of power and pride represented by the city and tower of Babel (Genesis 11:1–9). In the archetypal Babylon, people embarked on their own grand scheme; in Jerusalem there was an outpouring of God's Spirit in quite unexpected ways. In Babel, one language dominated to the exclusion of all others; in Jerusalem, a variety of languages continued to be spoken but there was communication between people.

Children are mentioned in Peter's Pentecost sermon (Acts 2:17–36), and when the new kingdom way of living started spreading among those who were baptized, children were obviously part of the new dynamics and processes. I have often tried to imagine how they felt—whether the increased communication and sharing between families threatened their security or whether they found the whole process exciting and fun. Perhaps, in the sharing that characterized the corporate life of the believers in Jerusalem (Acts 2:42–47; 4:32–37), it was children who were in the forefront of the hospitality, noticing new people who were in need and suggesting practical ways to help.

When communities face sudden new challenges and testings, children will often be ready to adapt and respond. Soon after the tsunami at the end of 2005, I was in Western India, leading a conference about Child Theology. Many of those present had been involved in responding to the tsunami in India and Sri Lanka. Towards the close of the day, I invited four or five groups to imagine a child standing on the shore after the tragedy, having lost absolutely everything—family, community, school, church, shelter and possessions. This little 'stranger on the shore' was destitute and orphaned. The groups were asked to distil their reflections into a single word. To our mutual astonishment, each group reached the same conclusion: the word was 'hope'.

When there are changes and challenges, even destruction, elderly adults may quite understandably find it all too much, but children often have the resilience and tenacity to respond without despair. Love must be able to weather storms, even those that engulf whole communities, and children are able to give as well as to receive love.

Group sizes

The Bible is a remarkable record of what happens to, within and between groups of different sizes. We have the Trinity (Father, Son and Holy Spirit), the group of twelve disciples that Jesus selected to be his closest followers; 70 or 72 believers sent out by Jesus on a mission; 300 troops selected by Gideon to fight a battle at night time; 3000 people converted at Pentecost; 144,000 as the symbolic number in the new Jerusalem. Jesus is specific about the essence of church: 'Whenever two or three of you come together in my name, I am there with you' (Matthew 18:20). A variety of groups and sizes is the norm.

Despite this, most Christians and church leaders assume that big is best and that growth in numbers represents success. I am much more taken by the SAS approach to matters. These specialist soldiers are given a task and asked to specify how they will go about achieving it, with particular reference to the best size of team needed. Different sizes of group are better suited to different tasks. You don't have to think long about this to realize how obvious it is: 'many hands make light work' but 'too many cooks spoil the broth'.

For this reason, and before we leave the subject of community, I want to pause to reflect on how size might affect the way children relate to communities. The child starts in a very small group (a dyad) and then, through family, is introduced to slightly bigger groups. Is there any rule of thumb that will help us consider what size of groups might be best for the growing child? Is there an ideal community size?

Children are very adaptable and will find ways of coping with any size of group, but I would ask that the child be given the chance to interact in a range of group sizes, with the proviso that there is a family group of less than a dozen in which the child is valued and feels at home, and that the age and life experiences of each child are taken into account.

Children must have the opportunity (without requesting it) to speak with a trusted adult at any time, as well as the experience of working as part of a team (two to, say, twelve, not forgetting rugby players!) and the experience of large celebrations (football matches, concerts, rallies and the like). You will find this range being worked out in most faith communities. The simple question is, 'How might love be encouraged to grow?' The size is right where a child feels safe and protected, and also able to play, to question and explore.

The child and others

As we noted at the beginning of this chapter, all groups exist because, in addition to being what they are, they are also *not* like another group. Our conceptual worlds tend to see 'us' as distinct from 'them'. That is not a good thing or a bad thing: it is the way things are. It mirrors the discovery of the child that there is 'self' and 'non-self'. The problems arise when there is conflict between groups, and history teaches that there always has been. There is a reciprocal process which starts by trying to help children develop reliable information about 'themselves' and 'others', and develops in such a way that they are encouraged to relate to others with sensitivity and appropriateness.

The Bible is a record of the origins of the Hebrews (a particular people known first as the children of Israel and later as the Jewish nation) and a group born from within this community, called Christians. It is therefore no surprise to find that the narrative is full of examples of the extraordinarily complex combinations of relationships and boundaries between these peoples and other groups. There are the descendants of Isaac and of Ishmael; there is the period when the Hebrews were slaves in Egypt; there are the relationships between this dynamic young nation and the peoples who already occupied the promised land; there are invasions by other empires; there are relationships between the Jesus-people and the Jewish nation, and between both groups and the occupying Roman forces. Children, of course, would have been in the thick of all this, and it is a fascinating exercise to try to imagine these events through the eyes of a child.

Jesus and the prophets invite hearers to see these relationships inside out, back to front and upside down, again and again. From God's point of view, all are one in Christ Jesus—Jews and Gentiles, male and female, slave and free (Galatians 3:28).

I want to make two main points here. The first is that little children, though needing to know who we mean by 'us', are also able to relate to 'others' more easily than many adults. There are probably many reasons for this, but one simple fact is that they are not so hampered by language: they communicate in a more universal language. Therefore, children may well be able to help us all in a globalizing world, if only we can find the settings and frameworks in which they feel comfortable and unthreatened.

The second point is that, as children grow, they discover that the world of relationships and people is not clearly defined. There are many variations and permutations. There are those who seem to be part of 'us' and 'them', but also those who are neither 'us' nor 'them'. Travelling communities and those deemed to have disabilities are two groups that are difficult to classify. There is ambivalence about such people and groups, and children find this as hard as adults do, if not harder. The Bible is insistent that all such people—specifically the widow, orphan and stranger—should be welcomed into the 'us' community. If children are not encouraged in this way while they are young, a pattern is set up and reinforced, and attitudes harden.

Family, church and schools all have parts to play in this process. If we could get over the notion that we have to teach children about such 'others' and realize that they have much to teach us, a whole new learning process would be set in train. This is not to say that children do not bully and abuse each other, but that there is a hidden dynamic waiting to be fostered.

Visions of a new community

Before we leave this scan of biblical insights into community, we should acknowledge the scope and scale of prophecies about new ways of living in the biblical canon. I commend them to you, particularly Isaiah, Zechariah, Micah and Revelation. They have much in common, including the fact that the new order is conceived in such a way that it is obviously a child-friendly way of living.

Some would regard this as utopianism, and I understand their concern. However, in our desire for practical outcomes and learning objectives, we must beware lest we shun visions. Without a vision, it is not just adults but also children who perish (see Proverbs 29:18, KJV). We could put it another way: in the fast-changing 21st century, what visions draw and illuminate our political and religious leaders? How do they compare to the biblical visions? It is not for nothing that this chapter is headed by a quotation from Zechariah, describing children playing in the streets of Jerusalem while elderly residents lean on their sticks and look on.

DISRUPTION OF COMMUNITIES

In previous chapters, we have reflected on what happens when the conditions for the growth of love are under threat—when children cannot find security, firm boundaries or a significant other person unconditionally committed to them. The loss of parents is one of the ways in which all three can be threatened at the same time, and sadly there are many ways in which the longing for an accepting community is also put at risk.

There are many ways of discussing the origins and effects of sin. One that may add substance to existing debates is to be found in

Stanley Grenz's *Theology for the Community of God*,[13] where he talks of sin disrupting communities. Grenz makes little or no reference to children, but here is an appropriate place, with children in our minds, to consider some of the consequences of the disruption of the communities into which many are born.

For many children, community life has been marred by poverty, but not so commonly understood is the way in which wealth, particularly associated with consumerism and individualism, has eaten into communities.[14] Children have suffered directly and indirectly in this process.

Then there is, for millions of children, the terrifying reality of war, in which communities are ripped apart and children are scarred for life emotionally, if not physically. Child soldiers are an awful feature of 20th- and 21st-century social life in parts of the world. I write at a time when many people are celebrating the 200th anniversary of the abolition of slavery—but one risk of this celebration is that we may be blinded to the many forms of child slavery flourishing now.

Famines, on top of chronic poverty, destroy communities. Some of the most harrowing biblical descriptions of cities focus on the way in which famine eats into social and communal life, causing people to act as barbarians, with mothers forced to eat their own babies. It is troubling that one of the most common images from the great continent of Africa is that of a dying child, with distended stomach and flies on his or her eyelids.

Perhaps the 20th and 21st centuries will be notorious not only for world wars, global warming and famines, but also diseases, notably HIV/Aids. For millions of children, the result of a combination of these disruptions is the collapse of family and community. Children are crammed into refugee camps or large institutions that resemble the very opposite of the visions of the great prophets and all that ordinary parents and neighbours long for. If we are talking about the growth of love, we must have something to say to these situations.

I have visited and lived in places of poverty in different parts of the world and listened to the stories of many of the poor. My response is to offer the themes of this book as some sort of starting point for all people, organizations and nations that seek to do something to help. We cannot, in my view, go to places with a ready-made template called adoption, fostering, family support, residential care, community development and so on. We must start from where children are, ask the fundamental questions about security, boundaries and significance and, from these, begin the embryonic communities that will sustain children and young people into the future.[15]

Having witnessed life in the slums of Mumbai, Manila, Sao Paulo and Kuala Lumpur, and townships in South Africa, I have campaigned for justice, and will continue to do so, with God's help, until my dying day. Yet in the slums I have encountered community, belonging and, yes, joy, which seems in very short supply in the affluent countries of the world.[16] If we are thinking about creating and nurturing communities, it is essential that we do not simply bring an affluent Western mindset to the issue. We are crippled by selfish individualism, which may have blinded us more than we know. Just as children may help us conceive of new forms of communal life, so those who live in poverty (including children and young people, of course) may have more wisdom and experience than we dare think about the nature of community.

Some years ago, I was at Spurgeons' College, where I have been teaching part-time for more than a quarter of a century. One of the students was from Albania. Her father was a professor of Marxist Maths. When the Albanian dictatorship fell, students at college were full of happiness for her. Things came to a head one breakfast time. She could no longer take the way in which her European colleagues were welcoming her and her country to their fold. She stood up and gave one of the most impassioned impromptu speeches I have ever heard: 'You have no idea what you are saying. You are selfish and miserable individuals with little or no understanding of real community and social relationships. Yes, we have gained some freedoms, but on balance I do not know as yet what I think. One thing we did know about was community and sharing. To lose this and become like you in the rest of Europe seems a very high price to pay for what you call democracy.'

The devastating effect that the disruption of communities has had on the lives of millions of children worldwide should cause us to rethink basic notions of belonging and community. I write as a Westerner but with a difference: I have lived most of my life among the rejected, poor and dispossessed. The community in which I live does not even figure on the mental maps of many social workers locally, but we have seen love grow, and we have experienced fun, play and joy together. That is perhaps why I see, in biblical visions and the expressions and dreams of others, models of life together that resonate with my own experience.

CONCLUSION: CEILIGHS

I would like to say a brief word about ceilighs—Celtic (or Gaelic) social gatherings, for which I cannot think of an English equivalent. They usually involve live music, dance, refreshments, speeches and jokes (the latter often at the expense of the English), but one element is so much taken for granted that it is rarely noticed: a ceiligh only merits that name if all generations are present. The grandparents may tell the stories or rock a baby in their arms; parents may lead the dancing and the band; children and young people will perform the sword-dance and other items. Crucial to the gathering is the presence of the whole community.

I used to live in Scotland, and that is where the way of the ceiligh sank in to me. I have sought to import it south of the border into our life at Mill Grove. It doesn't work perfectly—kilts and bagpipes aren't too popular, for a start—but you will see traces of the ceiligh in every aspect of our life together. We eat together, including the youngest and oldest, provided that they feel comfortable to be at the table with us; we have our prayers together; we encourage all age groups to enjoy the yearly festivals, notably Founders' Day, Harvest, Bonfire Night, Christmas and Easter. Holidays are events for all the family and we enjoy doing things like celebrating birthdays together. This is definitely not about adults entertaining children or vice versa: it is more about an event where a community celebrates together and every part of the community has a special part to play. All affirm and are affirmed, and there is solidarity of celebration.

If there is one overriding implication of the argument of this chapter, it is that communal worship, ritual and celebration are among the most significant elements of the life of a child.

Chapter Seven

CREATIVITY

We are God's work of art, created in Christ Jesus to live the good
life as from the beginning he had meant us to live it.

Ephesians 2:10 (JB)

DON'T YOU MEAN 'PLAY'?

As this book took shape in lectures and papers written and delivered
on all five continents, there were many questions asked and
comments made about content and style. One of the most common
suggestions was to call this theme 'play'. Students and colleagues
know how keen I am on play, and the books in this field usually use
that word. Yet there are many difficulties with the word 'play', in my
view, so I want to focus on the idea of 'creativity' instead. Let me
explain the reasons for this choice.

First, I want to encapsulate the essence of what it means for
children (like adults) to be made in the image of God. The thought
is expressed twice in Genesis 1: 'God said, "Now we will make
humans, and they will be like us…" So God created humans to be
like himself; he made men and women' (vv. 26–27). In my view,
the context is the key to the meaning of this rather mysterious
relationship. God is revealed primarily here as creator, so it follows
that we humans are little creators. It is our nature to shape, to find
meaning, to express thoughts in actions as well as words, to make
music and so on, so throughout this chapter I am thinking of
children as little makers, with the imagination that can conceive of

things being different and the ability to set about the transformation.

Second, 'play' is usually clearly defined in people's minds already. It is what children do when not in lessons. It is the opposite (or very nearly) of work. It is essentially non-productive. It has associations with playgrounds, games and toys. This is hardly surprising, and who could disagree? But do children distinguish between work and play in this way? Before writing this chapter, I went outside to cut some logs and store away the branches of recently lopped trees. My grandson Isaac joined me. As I ponder the things we did together, it is quite impossible to divide them into 'work' and 'play'. He helped me with some wood, putting it into the wheelbarrow. He carried other branches. He spent time in a little toy car. He sat in the barrow while I pretended it was a train and we went under the arches of some trees as if they were a tunnel.

I am reminded of one of my Swiss friends, who spoke to me of a childhood full of the tasks of survival high in the hills outside St Gallen. There was no time for formal play (that is, games), but everything the children had to do—whether in the kitchen, the dairy or the cowshed—they made into a game. Kristin Herzog makes a similar point: 'For a playing child there is no difference between creation and recreation, art and work, visions and re-visions of the world around it.'[1] The word 'creativity' avoids this false dichotomy between work and play.

Third, I want to express the fact that 'play' is probably the most sophisticated (adult) way of learning, teaching, writing (poetry is a special form of play, using words) and experimenting. At the limits of science, when the pioneers try to establish links between disparate concepts or worlds, their descriptions of what they do sound much more like play than hard work. A hypothesis is a form of play: 'Let's pretend A equals such-and-such, and imagine it in a different dimension'; 'Let's see what happens if we treat such-and-such as both a particle and a wave'; 'What if there is more than one universe?' and so on.

So, whether I use the word 'play' or 'creativity', I do not mean to suggest that we have left aside the world of education, work and school, or that we are talking about leisure pursuits only. Neither do I want to imply that the theme is inseparably linked to children and childhood and can be cast off when thinking of adults. The theme I am talking about includes all the play of children and childhood, and much more. It is about imagination, art, drama, music, therapy, sport, adventure, writing, poetry, sexuality, affection, and all the ways in which humans, physically or imaginatively, shape the world in which they live.

CREATIVITY AS THE ROOT OF HUMANITY AND RELATIONSHIPS

One of the reasons why I have eschewed the common idea of stages of child development is that, in this book, we are seeing growth in a more organic way. Now, as we put creativity at the forefront of our approach, we are, in part, revisiting ground that we have already covered, but from a new perspective. When thinking of attachment behaviour and theory, for example, we talked about the 'dance' between mother and child as a key to establishing the very first bonds of recognition and affirmation. There is a response of movement, gesture and eye movement between the mother and child. It is significant that Dan Hughes does not speak of a programmed or mechanical reflex response to describe this primary interaction: he uses the language of creativity and play. There is probably no better word than 'dance' to hint at the combinations of rhythm, movement, sound and touch in the mother–baby relationship. It is not about grammar, vocabulary or supply and demand so much as a spontaneous improvised drama. The mother is not always seeking improvements in the child, although she rejoices when they are in evidence. It is play for play's sake, and human relationships are warped in one way or another if, at heart, there is not a sense of enjoyment of each other's company.

Winnicott uses this idea as a basis for his understanding of psychotherapy (the therapist and the patient are playing together) and of cultural development in which play is the primary manifestation.[2] He sees psychoanalysis as bringing the patient from the state of being unable to play to a state where he or she can play.

CREATIVITY AND LANGUAGE

We do not have to make a very big leap to see how these first encounters between mother and child can pave the way for the discovery and development of language. When humans learn second or third languages, they may do so in formal ways,[3] but our first language is learned in a completely different way. It is fairly well agreed that language starts with movements, gestures and inflections rather than words. First there is communication in the form of the dance that we have already discussed. Next comes conversation in sounds without any words or grammar. This is a much underestimated phase, rather, to my mind, like the garden of Eden—a lost golden age.

When we arrive at the first books and phrases, it is play-like repetition that predominates. I stress the word 'play-like' because it is the opposite of learning by rote. In the latter, the teacher determines the subject and the order of things; in the former, it is the child who leads by making sounds and connections that appeal to him or her.

If you think of all the best books for very young children, you will see that, instinctively or by design, the writers play games with the reader, repeating patterns with variations so that the child becomes familiar with them. We might venture a rather obvious question that I haven't often heard: why does a young child return to the same book again and again, even in one sitting? He or she knows the content, so why the attraction? Is it not rather like a game? Every game, from tennis to Monopoly, follows certain patterns and abides by rules, but there are always subtle variations and the joy of the spectator and players lies in the variations. Perhaps it is so with the repeated reading of books.

The shape of the mouth, the expressions of the face, the position of the body—smiles, frowns and gestures—all contribute to what distinguishes one language from another, and it is a never-ending story. Stories become more elaborate and the language uses more metaphors and symbols. As I have mentioned, poetry is a form of conscious playing with words, and I feel that children instinctively prefer poetry to prose. Nursery rhymes may or may not be in decline, but their popularity surely lies in the imaginative games that are played with rhythms and sounds as well as with strange or common ideas.

Language does not make any sense without conversation, and it is interesting to ponder what comes first, the language or the conversation. I suggest that there is a game going on between them throughout. Spoken or written language is crucial to what it means to be human, to relationships and to social skills, and this essential component of human and social life has its origins in creativity—in a form of play.

CREATIVITY AND EDUCATION

We turn now to the subject of education and schools, and the place of creativity or play in them. A basic assumption is that work is what happens in classrooms, and play is what takes place in the playground (and outside school hours). This assumption matches the basic social division between work and leisure that is so crucial to the meaning of the lives of adults,[4] so we should not be too surprised if play is seen as superfluous to the real substance of education. It is about children letting off steam, so that they can get on with work again, and work means programmed learning: reading, writing and arithmetic. The whole edifice, even today in the

UK, is a very serious undertaking, girt with learning outcomes, lesson plans, assessments, progress checks, examinations and much more.[5] In the UK we are obsessed with outcomes compared with much of the rest of the world.[6]

There are many alternative philosophies of education, including those of Rousseau (described fully and with conviction in his novel *Emile*), Pestalozzi, Montessori and Fröbel, to name a few from Europe. All stress play and exploration as a key to learning. Children have a built-in sense of enquiry and movement, which shows itself primarily in questioning, testing and play. Sadly, these methods have been neglected in the UK and the USA and therefore in the rest of the world. Sadly, too, they are usually associated with preschool children, whereas, in fact, they are approaches to the whole of learning, whether in family or school, for children of all ages. What is more, they do not require school buildings. Imagine how well suited such an approach would be to most of the world—but the industrial model of education rules, OK?

I recall chatting with a head teacher of a school in India while walking through the grounds of a kindergarten. Some of her pupils were playing under a *gul mohol* tree. On closer inspection, I found that they had set up a cooperative factory in which they were collecting, categorizing, counting and packing nuts. They were completely engrossed in their collective endeavours so we could pause nearby without disturbing them. I observed to the teacher that here was real education and learning, and she responded without a moment's hesitation that this was not happening inside the school and therefore it could not be learning. I looked at her and, to my distress, saw that she was not joking: she was convinced that real education took place only in classrooms, behind rows of desks and with books open.

Learning can and should be derived from the basic interactions between a mother and child, and from the natural environment that gives the child the very essence of a sense of self, other and language. This kind of learning will connect with all the other aspects of a child's life, in family, faith community and the wider world—and the name I give to the predominant element and framework of this process is creativity.

All the moments when I made conceptual breakthroughs in my own schooling, as far as I can remember, derived from some form of connection with play, or a conversation with a teacher that was drawn from and led to experimentation. There was the English teacher who suggested alternative ways of telling the time with images and metaphors; the maths teacher who first revealed the links between a triangle and a circle; the art teacher who showed how colours combined to make new colours of the rainbow; the teacher who asked me what I liked about a poem and was honest enough to say that he hadn't seen that in it.

If we think of music in education, it only takes a moment to see that we talk about 'playing' an instrument—and that makes sense in that each interaction between player and instrument is an experiment, a conversation, a game of one sort or another. If the activity is merely mechanical, then it is not playing an instrument but simply being taught or doing exercises. Suzuki, if I understand him, is keen to allow pupils to express themselves, not without boundaries but with conviction.[7]

HUMOUR AND JOKES

You will have noticed that legislation, guidance, policy documents, bureaucracy and the like are completely devoid of humour. That is their metier, of course. If they started being witty, ironic or allusive, they would no longer serve their primary purpose.

On the other hand, you will have noticed that children are very fond of jokes and humour. Jokes are essential to growing children. I don't want to propound a theory of humour at this point (Freud and others have tried that), but it is worth noticing that humour allows children to cope with mistakes, difference, the vagaries of language and culture, misfortune, stress and tension.

I think that this is a particularly underestimated feature of childhood (Peter and Iona Opie were among the few who seemed to recognize its importance,[8] not least because they were determined to observe what children actually did and said rather than spelling out what they thought was good for children). We acknowledge the part that story plays in coming to understand self and others, culture and history, but we have missed the vital place of humour.

Research on resilience comes very close to acknowledging the role of humour: we know that resilience thrives where there is a willingness to rethink and reinterpret one's life story in the light of new insights into past and present. And what is humour if it is not about reinterpretation? It always involves some sort of pun or changed meaning in a word or situation: it sees things from at least two different points of view. Yet educational targets and guidance are about risk assessment, attainment of skills, protection: humour and fun don't get much of a look in.

Love is serious and is rooted in loyalty and commitment: it is not to be thought of light-heartedly. The growth of love is a painstaking process, but the fact is that in any friendship, including marriage, the partners will need to see the funny side of life if their love is to survive and flourish. Trees bend in the wind when there is a storm: otherwise they would break. There must be flexibility and suppleness coupled with their strong roots. Is it straining the analogy too much to think of humour as representing an aspect of this flexibility in human beings?

Humour and jokes represent some of the highest forms of communication within a culture or language. When learning a new language, we can count to ten very quickly; common vocabulary follows; specialist words and grammar take longer, but humour is the apotheosis of communication. When people can laugh together, then there is real community and shared understanding.

Why not try out this hypothesis: 'Children who genuinely see the funny side of life find relationships easier than those who don't'? The opposite is certainly true. I recall a girl who lived with us at Mill Grove, who had had a difficult home life even by our standards. One day, we were playing snooker while some other young people were playing table tennis nearby and laughing. She asked me in all seriousness, 'How do you know when to laugh?' I replied, perhaps too quickly, 'When you find something funny.' 'But how do you know something is funny?' she continued. I pointed out that she laughed sometimes (even if, I began to realize, with reserve and a little awkwardly). 'Why do you laugh when you do?' I asked. 'Because I see others laugh and know that is the right thing to do' she replied.

Then and there, it dawned on me that this girl had lacked any sympathetic and continuous setting in which she could possibly learn to understand what humans experienced and meant by humour. She was already a teenager, and it occurred to me that, like enjoying the taste of Marmite and olives, humour is perhaps only possible when learned at an early age.

Given that children were a part of many of the groups that Jesus addressed, I wonder whether they particularly appreciated the jokes in his stories and asides—the camel and the gnat, for example, or the plank and the speck of dust, the rich man and the eye of the needle. This might lead us to ponder how well we fare in many of our churches when it comes to jokes and humour. Perhaps the caricature of traditional church life and worship as humourless is closer to the truth than we would like to believe. In my life within a community and as part of a number of groups, I have come to see that the quality of relationships, trust and belonging is manifested most obviously and readily in a shared sense of humour. Humour is essential to group living and churches would do well to reflect on this fact.

THE BIBLE AND CREATIVITY

We started this chapter with reference to the image of God, so it is sensible to begin our more extended reflection with thoughts about his character and nature as revealed in the Bible. Richard Dawkins' summary of God's character as portrayed in the Old Testament, in his book *The God Delusion*, would give little reason to even consider God in relation to play and creativity,[9] but what would a more balanced description look like?

A few years ago, I led a retreat for a church in Cambridge on the subject of Child Theology. At the end of the long weekend, there was space for participants to share anything that they had seen for the first time or in a new way. A scientist explained how he had always known, as a Christian, that the temple curtain had been torn so that he might enter with confidence into the very presence of God through the death of Christ. During the conference, he had seen something quite remarkable: he was not only able to enter into God's presence, but God the Father was smiling at him. Indeed, God was not just smiling but beckoning him to draw nearer—and, more than that, to sit and play.

It was a complete reversal of everything this scientist had assumed: in the Holy of Holies, surely one could not play! Yet this was how he now saw God as Father. Immediately another participant shared that the day when the noise of children playing in the streets of Jerusalem is best heard is Yom Kippur, the Day of Atonement, the holiest day of the Jewish calendar. In the space created by the celebration of this festival, the children find it safe to play on the empty streets. Here was an echo of the first insight.

What evidence is there in the Bible for the idea that God is a playful creator? We might easily imagine a stern, scientific creator, but that is not what we are looking for. Here are some thoughts. It was suggested to me as a boy that God has a sense of humour, and we might think this through. Why the quite astonishing variety of colours, shapes and textures in creation? Is it all necessary, or is there a measure of playfulness at work? As one child put it, 'Dear God, Did you really mean for the giraffe to look like that?'[10]

The canon of scripture has some surprises for those who read the Bible without any expectation of imagination or humour. The book of Esther contains no references to God. The Song of Songs celebrates the joy of sexual love, as a manifestation of or metaphor for God's love. And what about Ecclesiastes? In arguing that everything is nonsense, this book requires the reader to see that role play is going on. We should be on our guard not to treat everything in the Bible in a wooden and predictable way; rather, we should respect the variety of genres and voices.

Jerome Berryman, who has done so much theological reflection alongside children, had chosen to call his approach 'Godly Play'. He is a playful person, and we need to bear in mind the games and allusions that he delights in. When he sets out the basic propositions of his theological position, he calls the first 'Peekaboo and the *Deus Absconditus atque Praesens*' ('the God who is hidden yet present'. He suggests that one way of understanding the relationship between God and his people is as a never-ending game of 'hide and seek',[11] and the fundamentals of this teasing relationship are there in the Bible for all to read—for example, at Emmaus when the risen Jesus disappears (Luke 24:28–32). Like Aslan in the *Narnia Chronicles*, we can never count on God to be present in a way that convinces us he is there. Perhaps this type of playful and unpredictable relationship is one of the best ways of describing both the nearness (the presence) and the absence of God.

If so, the parables of Jesus are in tune with this playful approach. In Matthew's Gospel, they focus on the kingdom of heaven, and this revelation of the way things are in the place 'where God has his way' is topsy-turvy and elusive. Just when the disciples of Jesus are convinced that they have it clear in their minds, he calls a child into their midst and says that unless they change and become like little children they will not enter this kingdom (Matthew 18:3). It seems upside-down, inside-out and back-to-front. R.S. Thomas' poem 'The Kingdom'[12] captures this elusiveness perfectly.

Perhaps the problem we have in understanding this idea stems from our conception of play: if we see play as trivial and unimportant, then we will consider it distasteful and possibly demeaning to think of God as playful. If we can understand play in the way described above, however, then a new way of seeing things begins to open up. It may be helpful to think of dance: perhaps God's relationship with us is to engage in an elaborate dance. The idea of conversation may help, too: our heavenly Father delights in playful conversation, wit and surprise.

We could, of course, think from a different angle and say that, because a sense of humour is unique to humans among the species on earth, this reflects the image of God.

All the time we must take seriously the savage reality of the suffering caused by sin, and the need for judgment, retribution and restoration. Given the brutalities of history, including the Holocaust and the mass deaths attributed to the policies of Stalin and Mao, how dare we introduce the concept of play into a discussion of God's character? There is no adequate response to such thoughts, whatever line we may take, but if God by his very nature loves to play, converse and dance with his children, it may be that one of the major disruptions of sin is to destroy the possibility of such a relationship. If so, we might see our adoption into his family as restoring the playful relationship between Father and child.

The description of the role of Wisdom in the creation of the universe in Proverbs 8:30 seems to suggest a playful joyfulness: 'I was right beside the Lord, helping him plan and build. I made him happy each day, and I was happy at his side.' Then, one of the visions of Isaiah portrays the kingdom of heaven inaugurated by the Messiah. It is a familiar passage, but perhaps we have not thought through some of its implications: 'Leopards will lie down with young goats, and wolves will rest with lambs. Calves and lions will eat together and be cared for by little children. Cows and bears will share the same pasture; their young will rest side by side. Lions and oxen will both eat straw. Little children will play near snake holes. They will stick their hands into dens of poisonous snakes and never be hurt' (Isaiah 11:6–8). The prophecy continues with judgment and refining to come, but at the core of the kingdom is a child playing in the company of animals, and the context is a dangerous one—poisonous snakes and no adult present.

The whole life of Jesus, for Christians, is a way to understand the very heart of God: we who have seen him have seen the Father. I recall seeing a performance of *Godspell*—a musical based on Matthew's Gospel. It seemed, to me, rather over the top and raised a number of theological queries, but I then reread the whole Gospel and found that a new side to Jesus' deeds and character had been unlocked. There was playfulness in so much of his teaching and his interactions with others. Sidney Carter captured this idea beautifully in his song 'Lord of the Dance'. If these interpretations are appropriate, then surely the life of Jesus reflects and embodies the heart of God.

We know, of course, that people did not all join the dance—that it ended in human tragedy—but that should not detract from what Jesus sought to do: to inaugurate a new way of living where there was life, fun, absurdity and improvisation. We have come to see life as very serious and, like the children in the marketplace (Luke 7:32), we don't want to join in either the dirges or the dances, but that is not the point. It seems to me that the dimension of play leads us into something very deep about the nature of God revealed in Christ. When we see children play, we may well be seeing more accurately into the heart of God than by other routes, and, if we see play as a key to learning, there is ample evidence to suggest that this might well be one of the preferred methods in the scriptures.

I have increasingly sensed that the parables that speak of the lost being found, with the subsequent rejoicing, reach into the very depths of things. If we insist on asking the age-old and compelling questions about how a God of love could create a world in which there has been such human suffering, one way of responding is to see that things and people become more precious after they have been lost and found again. This is not an answer—I do not believe we can expect one—but it does have the merit of hinting that there is more joy possible in the embrace of reconciliation than in any other embrace. There is 'more happiness in heaven because of one sinner who turns to God than over ninety-nine good people who don't need to' (Luke 15:7).

THE FIVE SENSES

Implicit in what we have considered so far is the way in which a child interacts with the material and social world by means of five senses (added together, perhaps they lead us somewhere near what may be meant by spirituality): touch, taste, smell, sight and hearing. It may be useful and even fun to note the way in which play provides an imaginative context or means of expression in each one. Of course, in reality they are combined (birth could be seen as the explosion that leads to a whole new means of experiencing the world, with sight and smell added to hearing, taste and touch) but for the sake of clarity we will separate them.

I am deliberately choosing not to describe Freudian or new-Freudian stages here (oral to anal and so on). This is not because they have no validity but because I am seeking to correct the notion of stages in child development as the ultimate framework of analysis.

Touch

We have explored the role of touch in the earliest attachment and bonding between mother and child. The contact with the mother's breast provides the vital milk, of course, but the contact between mother and baby is about much more than this. Touch continues the bonding that has been experienced for up to nine months in the womb, and the mother is soon aware that the baby is instinctively exploring her nipple and breast in a way that might be called playing.

Taste

Taste (difficult to distinguish satisfactorily from texture and smell) is focused first on the mother's fluids, but also the child's own body chemistry: saliva, sickness and various sorts of 'wind'. Over time there is an increasing variety of substances and flavours, and the basic likes and dislikes, known and unknown, may be established early on. (I have often wondered whether there is an age in a child's life, past which it takes a lot of practice and patience to enjoy things like sprouts, root ginger, sheep's eye-balls and the like!) The child will not treat eating and drinking as a simple functional exercise or routine, and it is not difficult to see how much play is going on in the process. Food is being felt, wiped on the head and hair, mangled and squeezed with the hands, dropped, sifted and so on. It is perhaps the primal form of 'clay' in the hands of the 'child potter'. There is no purpose in view (in the sense of deliberately making something) but the idea of play as experimentation helps to explain the little child's experience of taste.

Smell

I am not aware of research on the sense of smell in little children but I am sure that it exists and is integral to the bonding experience. Given its importance in other animals, it is likely to be not only associated with identity and belonging, but also acting as a trigger for emotions such as fear (for example, when a troubled mother gives off particular scents). My feeling is that smells are largely subconscious elements in the play of a child. If so, it is easy to see why they carry some of the deepest associations: they have not been so easily labelled as other sense data and so are able to work at a deeper and more integrative level.

Sight

Sight has been more widely studied: it plays an important role in the dance between mother and child, and, for those like Loder who see the critical role of the mother's 'face' in representing ultimate meaning, sight is a primary vehicle alongside touch for establishing consistent and reassuring responses. The all-important first reciprocal smile depends, of course, on sight, and we should note that one of the earliest games the child will play is a form of peekaboo—exploring the absence and finding of an object or a person. I think that this is the primary organization in little children's encounters with books: they are not looking for story and a coherence of the whole so much as particular objects, which they lose and then, when the page is turned, find again. This would help to explain why a child will return to the same page so many times, while the adult has a different frame of reference that relates to the story or classification, by type, number or colour of the objects represented in the book and so on.

Sound

The child is continually surrounded by sounds, many of them strange and raw, immediate and cacophonous, but some, like the beating of the mother's heart and the gentle words and humming of the mother, reassuring and comforting. The mother's heartbeat perhaps forms one of the sources for the bass and rhythm that make up the foundation of most music. If not striving to learn the meaning of particular sounds, which adults call 'words' and 'language', the newborn child is receiving a symphony of rustling, ringing, birdsong, running water, banging, sighing, snoring, animal noises and so much more. The composer Messiaen was not alone in seeing these natural sounds as the ultimate, the original and the ground of music, and human compositions as copying, simplifying and pointing to them.

As we have noticed, early speech is founded on very simple repeated sounds and rhythms. Nursery rhymes—songs with simple rhymes and rhythms—are part of the way in which children play not only with adults and peers but with themselves and the world of nature.

If we pause to consider recollections of childhood that ring true, we will quickly see how prominent these experiences of the senses are.[13] The senses will continue to be the vehicle for interaction with the world, coupled all the time with imagination and the search for congruence, meaning and completeness, but in early childhood they are not labelled and categorized by the child. It is possible to experience them for the sake of experience—as play or art, perhaps. Yet we can discern that the imagination and human interaction are responding to these spontaneous experiments and games in such a way that elementary types of meaning, in the form of patterns, are emerging. It is a process of adventure, like a voyage of discovery or the way artists interact with their chosen media in the earliest stages of their work.[14]

SAFE PLAY AND ADVENTURE

One of the challenges to child's play in contemporary societies is presented by what Ulrich Beck has termed 'risk society'—broadly speaking, the view of the world that conceives of risks as largely created by human collectivities, and the management of risk as an essential part of organizational life. Companies, schools, hospitals and charities are all familiar with the 'traffic lights' of risk assessment. At certain levels of operation, these assessments can make some sense, but, if we have children and their development in the centre of our thoughts, we find a fundamental problem. Children must take risks to learn anything: they will bump into things and fall over; they will completely misunderstand and miscalculate. A world purged of all risks and dangers would be so sterile that it would probably prevent children's growth and maturing.

From time immemorial, adults in parenting and teaching roles have tried to find ways of protecting children from undue risk and harm. In recent decades, there has been a growing body of evidence about dangers of which previous generations were unaware, including lead poisoning, carbon emissions, unhealthy diet, children without seatbelts in cars and so on. However, when a state, local authority or institution begins to produce policies on risk assessment and play, there is a fundamental and potentially irreconcilable difference of perspective and value. The corporate body will always tend to reduce risk to the point where growing children lose some necessary aids to development, not least the skill of managing risk and danger for themselves. It only takes one accident in Europe for there to be assessments of the causes, followed by policies and laws aimed at preventing a recurrence of the accident. No one can afford the risk of a child dying on a school trip, a coach accident, a tree falling over in the playground, injuries from games (whether football or conkers) and so on. The whole weight of expectations is on removing the dangers. But how can we find a proper balance with the need for adventure and play?

I have been discussing a new government policy for preschool children in England and Wales: these children are to spend at least 20 minutes each day in the open air. What progress! We are to have free range, or semi-free range, rather than battery children! I rejoiced —until I heard the next part of the guidance: the outdoor space must be safe to the point of sterility. Specifically, there must be no stinging nettles, no prickles, no sharp edges and no sun. I then grasped the essence of the policy: we were to try to recreate the outdoor world exactly in the image and mould of the safe indoor world. On balance, I wonder whether it might not be better to keep children inside at school, and let their parents allow them to risk contact with stinging nettles, brambles and sunshine at some other time of the day.

I guess it won't be long before trees are seen as too dangerous for all sorts of reasons: branches, conkers, acorns, pears and apples might fall down. If so, we would deprive ourselves of a situation in which Newton saw into the law of gravity! I am being ironic here because I wonder whether future historians will think we lost track of our senses somewhere along the line.

Obvious answers are to go for synthetic solutions and safe environments—so climbing walls will be preferred to rock faces, climbing frames to trees, smooth plastic toys to wood and stone, swimming pools to streams, inland lakes to oceans, and theme parks to genuine expeditions into the big outdoors. Virtual reality, as a replacement for the physical world, is a common experience for children: in virtual games they take extraordinary risks with 'themselves' and others, dying many times over. Such games are a substitute for real encounters with the material world.

In a nutshell, we are recognizing the dangers of 'safe play'. It may meet the demands of governing bodies for minimizing risk, but it does no service to children unless it is counterbalanced by a philosophy of life that is prepared for mistakes and accidents.[15]

What do I suggest for parents, teachers, churches and the like? Clearly there must be some attempt to raise the status of play so that it can be defended at every level. This is no mean feat, given its lowly current status, but the approach I commend is exactly what we have tried and tested at Mill Grove. In essence it is very close to the Montessori or Fröbel type of perspective. The adults have the responsibility for choosing the location, the terrain for the child's exploration. That choice must be made with care, taking account not only of the child's abilities and skills and the nature of the terrain itself, but also of the adults' skills, abilities, knowledge and familiarity with the location. This having been done, and with a minimum of tuition, the children are allowed to explore the chosen environment.

The adults remain near enough to help if things go horribly

wrong, but not so close that they stifle genuine encounters. A useful rule of thumb is that the adult should on virtually no account say the word 'careful'! The adult should not be anxious, or the anxiety will be communicated to the child. If the adult is worried, it is clear that the terrain is not appropriate. The onus is with the adults, but the responsibility then passes largely to the children and young people.

HOLIDAYS

Again and again, as I listen to people recount their childhood, holidays stand out. There are obvious reasons for this: people remember different places and new experiences. But what may be important is the way in which play and exploration become the concern and prerogative of everyone on holidays: play is shared. Adults and children take part together, if not equally.

If we use the word 'holiday' metaphorically or historically, we can see it as representative of those times when adults and children play together. These times are perhaps underestimated in the way we see children grow and develop. If we are trapped in a way of thinking that measures life by *chronos* (chronological time), then holidays are relatively unimportant compared to school terms, but if we are alert to the *kairos* (particular moments in time), holidays may well have their special place.[16] There may be times of shared activity: rowing in a boat together, climbing a peak, catching a fish, eating fish and chips on a harbour wall while the sun sets and so on, but I think holidays represent something more subtle. They are times when families are able to relate in ways beyond simple shared experiences.

In a biography of Lord Shaftesbury by Geoffrey Best, my eye caught the following sentence describing Shaftesbury, his wife Minny and their ten children at the seaside on an Easter Day: 'Minny and I... towards evening (took) a solitary walk on the sea-shore (while the blessed children ran about the sands) and recalled the past, and anticipated the future'.[17] I took it that the word 'solitary' meant there were no servants or friends present, so I imagined the scene—mother and father in earnest conversation while the children explored the beach without any interruption or guidance. It reminded me of the archetypal situation in which children seem to be happiest and most at ease—where there are significant adults present who are content together, have their own business or agenda, and allow the children to play and explore spontaneously. If the location of this cameo is outdoors, so much the better, for the opportunities for discovery and self-expression are likely to be enhanced.

It seems almost trivial to dwell on this type of scene, but I am convinced that it is of great importance for those of us involved in the welfare and care of children. To see why, we need to put sentiment and historical singularities on one side. In essence, the adults have (albeit unwittingly) created a child-friendly space for their children. They are not teaching or instructing the children; they are not playing with them or talking to them. Except in the broadest sense of awareness of their presence, they are not even conscious of what the children are doing. The children are safe and free to be themselves, relating to each other and to the physical environment as they choose.

I am not suggesting that we need to wait for and rely only on holidays to provide this child-friendly space but, if we can understand the special qualities of times spent together on holiday, we may be able to recreate some of them in everyday life.

If there is a single thing I have learned at Mill Grove over the years, it is that we need to find ways of creating space in which children can thrive without the adults necessarily doing anything with or for them. Many times I have discovered that, when husband and wife or grandparents are engaged in happy conversation or activity together, this creates just the right context for children to be creative themselves and to play imaginatively and contentedly.

WORSHIP

How does this relate to the issue of worship when children are present? I hope that readers can make most of the response to this question for themselves. Worship itself is a creative, perhaps playful response to God's initiative, invitation and grace. It is a mirror image or echo of the great act of creation. As such, it should evoke and find expression for all the deepest longings, stirrings, desires and feelings of the worshippers.

Children should be present at worship wherever possible, and what happens there should stir their imaginations and engage them at every level. It has been my privilege throughout my life to experience every kind of Christian worship in many varieties of denominations across the world, and I am not seeking to be critical of any one type. We need to give thought to providing space for children to stand, sit and kneel (yes, that is very important); the opportunity for them to hold a Bible and a hymn book themselves (this tactile experience is also important); the chance to be still, to speak, to sing, to play, to mime, to dance, to offer the bread and wine, to take the collection, to be part of the choir and so on.

When I see creative space being made for children, my soul sings, but when there is a mindless sort of pattern to worship that is patronizing or even despising, I become very angry. PowerPoint is often introduced into acts of worship without thought in an age when children are living in an electronically dominated and saturated world. We have special songs for them.[18] As I have already noted, most churches resolutely refuse to teach their children the Ten Commandments. Often, as a consequence of new technology, children are deprived of service books that they can hold and in which they can follow the worship for themselves. Many churches bar children from meetings and Holy Communion; parents often exclude them from funerals. I really wish it were not like this, but it is so, more often than I can bear to think.

When we see children and young people in creative settings, like ceilighs, the full range of their creativity and play can be expressed in their own way and their own time, enriching us all. When I think of the times I have been moved by the participation of children in worship, I realize that it has happened in every sort of way—through reading, singing and dancing. The dancing of children in the Philippines always moves me to tears. What is it that evokes this deep response? I think it has to do with respect for them, the excellence of what they are doing, and their joy and commitment.

Many years ago, I agreed to take an elderly teacher of mine to a school concert on the other side of London. The teacher who was conducting had been one of her former pupils at our school, Leyton County High. It was an act of respect and kindness on my part, and I was feeling rather good about doing it. As we sat in the front row of the school hall, however, I wished that the event had been something a bit better. After all, what options for entertainment there were in London every night—and here we were, awaiting a school choir. Then suddenly there was a moment of truth. The conductor, Russell Burgess, came to the rostrum. It was like an extraordinary revelation: electricity seemed to pass through the choir as it stood up.

You might say that standing up isn't very creative. Well, let me tell you, in a split second I realized that this was no ordinary choir. I was in the presence of greatness. It was the famous Wandsworth School Boys' choir. Their musicianship was outstanding, and yet for the most part they were ordinary boys who had been guided and shaped by one of the most remarkable chorus masters of his time. What an evening! Ever since, it has been clear to me that we often do not create the space for children's potential to develop to anything like its full extent.[19]

Sunday school, or children's church, as well as the rest of church life, is simply selling children short, and yet it has the potential to do so much. We have settled for mediocrity when God has given the potential for excellence. It may be that this shortcoming reflects an assumption that children are incomplete adults and therefore cannot be expected to produce anything excellent. Indeed, they will produce sounds, pictures and creations that are different from those of adults, but this does not mean that they are inferior. It is not a matter of putting pressure on them, but of creating the space and expectations that enable them to give of their very best.

SPORT

It would be strange to have a chapter on creativity (play) without some space being given to the subject of sport—organized physical games. Football is hugely popular with children worldwide, and most will be expected to take part in some form of sport as part of the school curriculum. Some children do not like sport: some feel intimidated and threatened by it. Sensitivity is therefore required in this area as in everything else. For those who do enjoy sport, however, it is a very good way of learning a combination of skills, including boundaries, self-expression and training, teamwork, the acceptance of losing and winning, and playing in a defined space and way. It is my experience that those who do not take part enjoyably in sport (or in other organized games, such as chess) can be socially handicapped as a result. The social skills needed to operate in everyday life are, in some ways, being role-played in sport.

There is also a beauty to be found in every sport beyond mere function and technique. I invite you to think of some of the games of tennis player Roger Federer: I find it impossible to describe how he plays without recourse to the language of aesthetics.

SUMMARY

Creative play is potentially one of the most important activities in the life of a child, yet it is rarely given the attention it deserves.

Love is about giving and taking, losing and finding, laughing and crying, birth and death, engagement and separation, and so on. In one way or another, all of these aspects of love are experienced in childhood through imaginative play and creative activity. But we are not only talking about preparation for future adult relationships. Through play, children are really loving and being loved. For those who know it, *The Velveteen Rabbit* has much to teach on this theme.[20] Toys are loved; characters in books are loved. Pets are loved—and the way the death of pets is handled is very important.

In order for us to take play seriously enough, it has to be rethought, and that requires an act of imagination and will. Parents and church communities may be able to provide models for others. It is unlikely that progress will be made through policy statements and guidelines.

All the time, perhaps Peekaboo was one of the overarching themes of history: 'I was lost but Jesus found me…'

❖

Chapter Eight

HANDS TOGETHER

Teneo et Teneor ('I hold and I am held')
The motto of Spurgeon's College

We have come to the end of our reflections on the five themes, and can perhaps imagine using the five fingers of a hand as reminders of them, making some symbolic connections.

- The thumb is critical for gripping and for security.
- The index finger is used for pointing and may symbolize boundaries rather nicely.
- The middle finger is the biggest and is therefore a good reminder of significance.
- The fourth finger sometimes wears a wedding ring and speaks of covenant and community beyond the immediate family.
- The playful little finger is last but not least.

I invite you to explore or reject this idea depending on your temperament. Be that as it may, we have used only one of our two hands. Have we nothing to say about the other hand? In thinking about the nature and context of the growth of love, we have focused on children and have considered the five major factors in facilitating or undermining a child's capacity to give and receive love, but what we have been considering is, of course, not restricted to children. We have been thinking about human development and exploring the nature of love itself. So we have elements of an anthropology in which we are trying to distil some of the features of what it means to be human, whatever our age, gender or culture, and to enquire into what best nurtures our desire to love and be loved.

THE OTHER HAND

This is the point where we come to the other hand. It can be seen as representing the 'significant others' in a child's life—both adults and children. If the needs, hungers and desires of these others are not in some way met, then their capacity to give and receive love to and from children will be impaired. For example, a person who is insecure or not good at recognizing and keeping appropriate boundaries is likely to be a hindrance to the growth of children and possibly even a danger.

All of us are found to be incomplete when our personalities are scrutinized with reference to the five themes. The experience of complete inner security is very rare. Jesus was able to sleep soundly in a boat while a storm was terrifying his disciples (Mark 4:38), and the apostle Paul wrote, 'I have learnt to be satisfied with whatever I have' (Philippians 4:11), but few Christians have attained that level of inner peace and security. For most of us there are situations and personality types that trigger defensive mechanisms and responses.

We could work through each of the five themes in a similar vein. Who is perfect in their recognition and respect of boundaries, for example? Who is fully aware of and secure in a sense of their own significance and self-worth at all times? Who is fully and appropriately part of social groups and communities, always mutually enriching? Which of us is completely creative and playful in every area of our lives?

Given these shortcomings, how do we assess which adults are 'good enough' to be entrusted with specific or direct parenting roles? The five themes may provide a useful ready reckoner to add to existing biometric and psychological models. A particular insight is that people may be drawn to children (a common phrase is 'I love children') precisely because of their own sense of incompleteness. In short, they may be seeking to meet their own needs at the expense of the children they purport to help, and projecting their own feelings on to the children.[1]

People lacking in self-worth for whatever reason may seek to work with children because they see them as vulnerable, helpless, trusting, receptive and non-threatening. In the process of trying to help children seen in this way, these people may feel more significant, important and valued. They gain self-esteem because they are helping a poor, helpless child. In the process, they may well create a dependency relationship in which the child continues to rely on and need them. Deep down, such a person doesn't really want the child to grow up, to answer back and to become an independent agent.

Likewise, people who have difficulties in personal relationships (whether as part of a group or member of a community) may be unconsciously drawn to a residential community of children or a school. They hope that such places will be safer and easier, with clearer guidelines and not so much reciprocity. They are looking for a safe harbour, with a reduced risk of being made to feel exposed and vulnerable.

In fact, such communities are more like rough seas. Children are not sentimental, kind, loving and so on; they are like all human beings in having a mixture of characteristics and emotions, and those who are vulnerable, insecure and lacking appropriate internal boundaries will need to test and try adults who seek to come alongside them. Children in these circumstances are the opposite of forgiving. Most of us have witnessed or been part of a class that has found ways of getting round a teacher, and we know what happens when the class is out of control. There is very little obvious and expressed sympathy for the teacher. In fact, children in groups may be particularly cruel.

Some readers of this book may have become aware of their own life story and needs in a new way. If so, they should seek to find ways of addressing the issues that arise. It may be that some are unsuited to work with children; it may be that others in a household, school, church or community can compensate for our weaknesses and vulnerability. The way forward is not to continue oblivious to our personal needs, but to turn to others who can help with realistic assessment and support.

I am grateful to Jo-Joy Wright for the way in which she has developed some of this thinking based on the five motifs, in an unpublished paper she has generously shared with me: 'A Model of Ways of Assessing and Addressing Workers' Needs'.[2]

TWO HANDS

With one hand there are many possibilities, but with two these possibilities are multiplied many times. One of the features of classical Indian dance is the importance attached to the hands and feet, fingers and toes. It is not just the legs, arms and body that move, but each digit, in very intricate patterns and shapes.

Imagine two hands, with each finger functioning well in and of itself and also as part of the hand, and picture the dance that is possible simply between the two hands, using all the fingers. We can see this as symbolic of a beautiful dancing relationship between people, from the exploratory play of toddlers as they find out what their fingers can do, right through to romantic love between two human beings.

Using fingers and hands, it is possible to role-play various interactions between a child and an adult. A tightly closed hand can represent a withdrawn child, perhaps depressed and angry. (You can imagine such a child, perhaps closing one of your hands so tightly that it is uncomfortable or even painful.) I sometimes invite a member of a class of students to use one of his or her hands to interact with my closed hand (the symbolic child), as a way of representing how they might go about the process of coming alongside and helping the child. When using this model, I have been surprised by the way some adults react. They have deliberately taken hold of one of my fingers and begun to prise the hand painfully open. I have wondered whether some were resisting the urge to smack the closed hand, or whether some would like to knock for attention.

If you think of all the resources represented by a caring hand, you can immediately see the possibilities of empathy, sympathy, affirmation, comfort and play. You can stroke the back of the hand or a single finger; you can hold the hand tenderly; you can tap rhythms on the hand; you can role-play the hand. Touch and the holding of hands can therefore be used as a practical way of understanding the potential interaction between an adult and a child.

How might caring and concerned adults go about dealing with the personal brokenness and incompleteness in their own lives, as a way of equipping them better for relating to children? We can approach this issue in many ways, including the use of child protection training, but here we will work through the five themes briefly in a practical way.

We must recognize throughout that there is a special place for the wounded healer and the use of vulnerability.[3] The search for the complete, fully mature adult is fruitless: being alongside or living with children will expose raw nerves, anxiety and pretension, just as water inevitably and inexorably finds its way through the smallest crack in the hull of a boat. A measure of self-awareness, demonstrated by and laced with humour, is perhaps one of the keys to good enough parenting.

By reflecting on adults drawn to work with children in relation to each theme we have a simple way of assessing aspects of the adult's character and personality.

Hands together: security

One of the games we play at Christmas at Mill Grove is called Skittles. Participants gather round a number of wooden skittles placed at random on the floor, and hold hands. When the circle is complete, the object is to attempt to pull the two people either side of you on to one or more skittles, so that they knock them over. All the time, you have to be careful not to knock the skittles over yourself, as the people either side of you are also trying to force you on to the skittles. The game proceeds until there is only one person left who has not knocked over a skittle or let go of the hands of the person next to them. It looks like a version of mayhem, but there is a lot of skill that goes into survival.

Crucial to success is a firm grip. As the game progresses, hands get tired and there is a lot of perspiration, which makes holding on ever more difficult. There are various ways of gripping safely or securely—a sailor's grip, a double grip involving grasping each other's wrists and so on.

All these grips are variations on the theme of *teneo et teneor*. You need to know that if, for any reason, you lose hold of a person, that person has still got hold of you. If we transpose the scene to a rescue on a mountain or in the sea, things immediately become clearer: a firm grip can mean the difference between life and death. So we can think of a way of holding hands that is fundamentally about security. What is necessary is the hold that will not let you go. There are times when nothing else will do; nothing else is remotely relevant. Fingernails might bite into and even pierce the skin; a grip may bruise the other person, but the hold is secure.

The hold represents the essence of attachment and bonding: the relationship is secure. Adults considering helping children would do well to reflect on experiences of 'holding' in their own lives.

Holding hands: boundaries

Shaking hands is a common form of greeting in many parts of the world, and probably has its roots in cultural, trading and even military traditions. It represents a way of communicating a meeting of two people who are probably not from the same family, who accept boundaries of culture and place, perhaps rank, and express a willingness to communicate across these boundaries.

Most sports involve a handshake. It marks not only the start or finish of a game, but also the end of one form of relationship (say, knocking up) and the beginning of the real thing, when two people are opponents. At the end of the game, when one is victorious, there is a handshake that represents the fact that it was a game. Both players are still alive and can continue, if not as the best of friends, at least as acquaintances—not locked for ever in combat.

Likewise, a handshake has been used as a way of setting a seal on a deal in business or politics. It is likely that there will be documents to be signed, but the handshake is a visible way of showing that new boundaries have been established: something has changed, and the agreement will be respected.

In some wedding services, the bride enters on the arm of her father or his representative, who 'gives her away'. Her hand is then placed into the hand of her future husband. These hands of the married couple are blessed by the minister, symbolic of the joining of their lives until death. After the wedding service the parents of the bride and groom leave holding hands in arranged pairs: the bride's father with the bridegroom's mother; the bride's mother with the bridegroom's father. The message is a consistent one: a whole new set of relationships (that is, boundaries) has now been established as a consequence of the joining of the hands of the bride and groom.

Adults considering helping children should explore times and experiences in their own lives when boundaries have been appropriate and inappropriate.

Holding hands: significance

One of the ways in which lovers show their affection for each other, and not coincidentally to others, is by holding hands. In some ways, this is a renegotiation of boundaries: we don't normally hold hands, and now we acknowledge mutual affection and significance. There can be much tenderness and expression given through this coming together of hands. There may be a gentle squeeze to show a shared feeling or observation, a soft stroking, fingers entwined.

When a person is grieving, hurt or bereaved, a common form of touch is to hold hands. Once again, the touch is symbolic of a whole relationship or emotional response. The hands of the distressed person may be enfolded or one hand held reassuringly. The gesture may well say more than any words can at this time. The message is that another person has come alongside, remains alongside and understands something of what the other is going through: 'I know what you are experiencing. I do not have a magic wand to wish away your loss and pain, but I am with you in it.' It is not a written or electronic message. It is personal, involving physical contact.

Adults helping children should ponder how and why certain people in their own lives have been especially significant to them.

Holding hands: community

The reflection on the meaning of hand-holding at the wedding service is in some ways an expression of community—a sense of belonging beyond the marriage relationship and immediate nuclear family. This is necessary for neighbourhoods, tribes and peoples to function effectively.

In some churches there is a service of membership in which a person is 'given the right hand of fellowship' by the leader(s). It is a holding of hands that symbolizes the joining of a community.

Likewise, when 'the peace' is given in a church, there is often the holding of hands. Here the symbolism is very clear theologically and socially. Jesus Christ has given a unique peace (*eirene*) to his chosen followers, which exists not only within each of them but between them. It is a bond that unites this particular community.

The clapping of hands is a simple but very effective way for a group to celebrate a particular experience or event together. Here the hands are not held but, by making a sound together in the same place and at the same time, the group expresses its solidarity and common mind. The clapping of hands to music is an aspect of the same process.

We have thought of Indian dance when focusing on the significance of fingers and touch. Much traditional dance in the UK involves groups—pairs, fours, eights and more—holding hands and thus expressing the subtlety of relationships within the wider community. Dance is historically a way of representing community solidarity, with the holding of hands symbolizing the bond between an individual and the whole.

One of the ways in which communities often express themselves is by holding hands around a special space. This has happened in different places around the world. The women of Greenham Common did it around a weapons establishment, and it happened at Jubilee 2000. The joining and linking of hands around a special site represents a community expressing its feelings about belonging and control. When police link hands to form a boundary, it is a very specific form of this expression, but where there is no desire to do anything by force, the linking of hands is a powerful sign of human belonging and aspirations. Where children are part of the 'human chain', the circle represents not only the whole community now, but also its significance through time and generations.

Adults intending to help children should assess the nature and quality of their relationships in the groups of which they are a part.

Holding hands: creativity

In a way, we return now to the place where we started this chapter. Creativity is not a separate and discrete aspect of life, divorced from security, boundaries, significance and community, but a way of expressing, imagining and experiencing all these things.

The holding of hands in play is everywhere to be seen in a variety of forms. Some of the very earliest interactions between parent and child, accompanied by rhythm and music, involve playing hands: think of 'Round and round the garden like a teddy bear', 'This little piggy went to market', 'Here's the church and here's the steeple' and so on. Then there are games like cat's cradle, and the rather risky one where the contestants try to trap each other's thumbs. Such games model cooperation and contest, two of the coordinates of social life.

In games such as netball and basketball, a ball is passed by hand; in marbles, a transitional object is moved from one set of hands to another. Skipping, relay races, tag and so on all involve a playful interaction where forms of touch are central to the meaning of the whole activity. One form of 'hide and seek' involves an increasingly large group, holding hands and spreading out across a playground or open space, seeking to enfold (capture) others.

In dramatic performances, not least puppet shows and mimes, hands have a very special role. Every human emotion can be expressed in some way through drama as well as through dance in its many forms—classical and modern, choreographed and spontaneous.

It may be worth pausing to consider the representation of the holding of hands in painting and sculpture. The gap between the hand of Adam and the hand of God in Michelangelo's painting in the Sistine Chapel—and the contact that we imagine to take place next—in some ways captures sacred and human history. The popular representations of praying hands are an unintended response to this gap: human hands are placed together in an archetypal posture of prayer.

Adults who hope to help children should normally be able to express themselves in one or more of these creative ways.

As we reflect on the holding of hands, it is possible to imagine the hand or hands of a little child or children. A good place to end may be with the vision of Martin Luther King in his great speech: 'I have a dream that one day, down in Alabama, with its vicious racists, with its governor having his lips dripping with the words of "interposition" and "nullification"—one day right there in Alabama little black boys and black girls will be able to join hands with little white boys and white girls as sisters and brothers.' Perhaps in this vision we see how the holding of hands can encapsulate much of what we mean by the growth of love.

HOLDING HANDS IN THE BIBLE

If this symbol of hands proves useful, it is worth exploring the role of hands in the Bible. Here are some examples of what we find. In the Old Testament, there is Eve holding the fruit she has taken from the forbidden tree in the middle of the garden of Eden, and Adam's acceptance of the fruit from her (Genesis 3:6). There is the elderly and partially sighted Isaac feeling his younger son, Jacob, who has disguised himself with goatskin to feel like his hairy brother: 'your hands feel hairy like Esau's' (27:22). Moses holds up his hand to part the Red Sea (Exodus 14:21). In Leviticus, the priest lays both of his hands on the live scapegoat, confessing over it the sins of the people before sending it into the wilderness (Leviticus 16:21). Gideon chooses only those men who use their hands to drink water to be part of the 300-strong army that will enter battle with him (Judges 7:6–7). Then there is the clapping of hands to celebrate the crowning of a king (2 Kings 11:12).

At the end of his encounter with the living God, Job places his hand over his mouth as a sign that he regrets having spoken out of turn (Job 40:4, NIV). The Psalms often use hands as a symbol of

God's presence, care and protection: see, for example, Psalms 37:24; 44:2 (NIV); 45:4 (NIV) and 98:1 (NIV). In Isaiah, the young child puts his hand into the snake's nest while playing and is completely safe (Isaiah 11:8). God's hands are instruments of creation and judgment (40:10–12, NIV). Our names are engraved on God's hands (49:16, NIV).

In the New Testament, Jesus takes little children into his hands and blesses them by placing his hands on them (Mark 13:16). Cutting off a hand is preferable to offending God morally and spiritually (Matthew 18:8). At God's right-hand side is the place where his people are called to be and to know they are safe for ever more (25:33–34). Jesus takes the hand of a twelve-year-old girl, whom family and friends believe to be dead, and tells her to get up (9:25). In the same community, an unclean woman touches him and he encourages her to admit that she has done so (Mark 5:27–30).

The hands of Jesus taking bread, blessing and breaking it, have a great significance in the Gospels (for example, Luke 22:19; 24:30), and on the cross Jesus shouted, 'Father, I put myself in your hands!' (23:46).

Touching is specifically mentioned after the resurrection of Jesus (Luke 24:36–43; John 20:17). Thomas, known as the doubter, will for ever be recalled as the one who said he would not believe until he saw for himself the nailprints in the hands of Jesus, and to whom Jesus said, 'Put your finger here and look at my hands! Put your hand into my side. Stop doubting and have faith!' (John 20:27). The laying on of hands was a special feature of the way the early Christians expressed their faith in God's power to heal and save (Acts 6:6; 8:17; 13:3; 19:6; 28:8). Paul ends his letter to the Colossians by writing with his own hand (Colossians 4:18), and, finally, lifting hands in prayer is common throughout the scriptures (for example, 1 Timothy 2:8).

This is a far from exhaustive list but it is enough to show that if we seek to draw from the Bible in order to focus on hands as symbols, we have a rich treasure store.

SUMMARY

In using hands as symbols of human life, growth, experiences and relationships, we find that they are wonderful but simple resources, as visual and tactile aids. Hands are also used in the Bible to portray not only human relationships but also the encounters between God and his people.

Guidance I was reading recently about child protection in schools (covering teachers with children as young as four years old) mentioned that it is 'unrealistic to expect a teacher not to touch pupils in the course of the learning process'. There was nothing about the positive aspects of touch at all, only the worry about how any touch might be wrongly interpreted. Do we really live at a time when the incidence of—or our obsession with—physical and sexual abuse has reached such proportions that we would prefer children to spend most of the day without the reassuring touch of caring adults? If so, what does this mean for us and for our children?

It may be argued that this document was about child protection and should not be seen as representative of our whole approach to child care. If so, we may wonder where is the corresponding evidence of guidance celebrating the gift of touch. Furthermore, what do we mean by child protection if a little child crying because of pain, separation or fear cannot rely on supportive and caring hands being placed around his or her shoulders or taking gentle hold of his or her hands? What are we protecting children from if, in the very process of trying to minimize the risk of physical and sexual abuse, we deprive them of the fundamental security for which they long, and which is so often, in human relationships, expressed through hands?

❖

Chapter Nine

HANDS APART

The worst disease in the world today is not tuberculosis or leprosy... It is the poverty born of a lack of love.

Mother Teresa

In this chapter we identify some of the factors that prevent the harmonious coming together of the hands that symbolize the sensitive and positive relationships between 'villagers' and children. This may seem a rather depressing prospect, but the intention is to explore what an agenda for action on behalf of the world's children would look like if facilitating the growth of love were at its heart. The current situation is not fixed and immutable. Concerned and committed 'villagers' can be part of a process of change, and this chapter may help us to clarify potential roles and responsibilities in shaping things for the better.

The focus is on ten of the worldwide threats, direct and indirect, to the growth of love in relation to children today and in future generations. These ten threats are preceded by a general point about a change in consciousness concerning children and childhood. (There may be some surprises in what follows because we are used to more well-tried categories of the major problems involving children, such as infant mortality due to malnutrition and poor water, child soldiering, sex trafficking in children, HIV/Aids and so on.)

THE COMPARATIVELY LATE 'DISCOVERY' OF CHILDHOOD

If we compare our understanding of women, former colonial subjects and those who live below the poverty line with our understanding of children and childhood, it can be convincingly argued that the world has noticed the universal 'social continent of children' late in time. We were not previously unaware that children existed, of course, but we did not see them, study them and respond to them in their own right. In sociology they tended to be subsumed within categories such as family, poverty, socialization or education. The 1989 UN Convention on the Rights of the Child marked a sea change in attitudes in this respect, and since the 1990s the sociology, theology and politics of children and childhood have begun in earnest.

In some ways this discovery is a blessing, but its late arrival means that the world has been developing at a rapid pace and trends have become traditions: some seem like fixed points. Some of the factors listed below have long been a threat to the well-being and growth of love in children. Had we recognized them earlier, we might have been able to challenge them; now it is unclear how we can take relevant and practical action.

A concrete example in Europe is the decline in church attendance and engagement that includes children and young people. It is estimated that over 30 per cent of local churches in the UK now do not have a single child or young person in them. Sunday school attendance, which was so important for generations, whatever the beliefs of the parents, has dwindled to the point where it is a minority pursuit. While this decline was happening, there was virtually no theology of childhood and related work going on. Ministers were being trained in colleges without any reference to children. Church life, worship and mission marginalized children and those adults who worked alongside them.

Now there are signs of life in this whole area, with the Child Theology Movement, a growing collection of significant books on theologies of childhood, Godly Play, plans for a children's ministry degree in the UK and so on. Yet one of the challenges is how to apply this knowledge in the situation that has developed: these shoots of life seem to have come in the winter rather than in the springtime, when there were far more children and young people in churches.

TEN THREATS TO THE GROWTH OF LOVE

Liberal democracy

Liberal democracy may seem a strange place to start in global terms. It could be said to offer more for children than some of the alternative regimes around the world,[1] but let us stand back for a moment and ask 'What is the essence of liberal democracy?' It is a political process based on the fundamental right of individual adults to choose their government through the ballot box. There is much debate about what is meant by a civil society, the public sphere and so on, but at its heart is the individual adult who is deemed to have certain rights.

When liberal democracy was born as a system in Europe and America, it was set in particular political, social and religious contexts.[2] The concept of an 'individual' in the current sense did not exist: it was assumed that every person lived within settings and groups in which there was a prior commitment to the good and well-being of that group. These settings included marriage, family, work, religious commitments, community and voluntary organizations.

We live in a completely different context now, in which (even though no individual can survive as an island) the philosophical concept of an individual and the focus on the rights of this individual have come to dominate our thinking and our political world. Whether we like it or not, this emphasis must undermine the rights of groups and associations: it is a zero sum game where an increase in the rights of one part of the system will mean that the rights of other parts will be reduced.

Clearly, there are real gains in the process, as individual self-expression is encouraged and the domination (or even oppression) of work, family and community is lessened. However, this form of democracy is very young and may not spread, or even last, in the form in which we know it.[3] One of its problems is the way it disenfranchises children and young people. There was a time when only the head of a household voted (the head being male). Then women gained the vote in most parts of the world, and so we talk of 'universal suffrage' while specifically excluding young people. So far there has not emerged a satisfactory way of including them, directly or indirectly.

There is much talk now of the rights of children and their 'agency', but the heart of the democratic system excludes them. Dare we not consider a children's parliament or a youth parliament? After all, there are school councils and church-based youth cell groups, and various organizations have 'shadow children's committees'.

Liberalism

As a political philosophy, liberalism is distinct from liberal democracy but closely allied to it. A liberal democracy might elect a conservative or socialist government, for example, that would not necessarily agree with liberalism. Liberalism stresses individual rights, freedom of thought, limitations on the power of governments and religions, the market economy, free private enterprise and the free exchange of ideas.

If you consider this list, you will immediately notice that children are absent. You might go on to say that, obviously, children would benefit from living in a society where liberalism held sway. There are indeed many benefits, compared with more traditional societies, but there is a hidden downside that is rarely exposed. Take the free exchange of ideas and how that idea relates to children.

It is axiomatic that children need protection, and this protection includes the censorship of visual and written information. That censorship is represented by bans on certain forms of advertising during children's programmes on television, a TV watershed intended to guard what children watch before they go to bed, the rating of films and the placing of 'adult' materials on separate shelves in shops. There are few who would argue that everything that circulates on the internet, for example, is suitable for children.

So it is generally agreed that censorship is necessary in order to preserve our understanding of childhood. What guidance does liberalism have to give about this? It will generally be applauding attempts to make material available that has been traditionally banned and suppressed, so where and how does it draw the line? All over the world, concerned parents, community leaders and pastors plead for something to be done about the negative effect that 24-hour television is having on the lives of children. The typical response of governments and corporations is to say that the TV can be turned off but, as technology makes possible the downloading of material on to increasingly cheap devices, and good enough parenting is far from universal, this is naïve.

While the prevailing philosophy of liberal democracies is liberal in this sense, children and childhood are endangered and there is no adequate framework for a response.

Education

While the world applauds universal education as the best thing that we can do for our children, and with the Prime Minister of Great Britain elected in 1997 with a mandate that he called 'Education, education, education', it might seem strange that the subject should be considered as a 'threat' to the growth of love.

Once again, as with liberal democracy and liberalism, there are real gains and benefits in the education system, but what are the prevailing philosophy and values of education? Along with radicals like Paulo Freire and Ivan Illich, I am concerned about formal education at a fundamental level. On balance, I encourage children to go to school (and I have sent my own children to schools) but we must keep up our guard and seek for the best.

Schools are set up by adults (remember that liberal democracy, like all other systems of government, is run by adults) and administered by adults. One of the objectives is to communicate knowledge and develop skills in prescribed areas or subjects. The adult/child dichotomy is inherent in the whole process: schools are there to aid the development of mature citizens and workers. They are like a banking system, where societies invest in children for expected returns.

At the same time, the word 'care' is seen to be about everything except education: teachers teach and parents care. School is for learning and home is for caring. We can see this clearly in the institutional divide between education and care in the state system for 'looked after children'. So how does schooling fare in relation to the growth of love? Where is love on the agenda? What about security, boundaries, significance, community and creativity?

Unchecked formal education will seem to be, at worst, neutral in all this. However, with preschool nurseries in Britain being inspected by Ofsted and judged by learning outcomes and risk assessments, the future does not look bright for schools as communities where there is play and fun—as moral communities where the present is not always seen in the light of the future and 'progress'.[4]

I have witnessed formal education systems in different parts of the world, where diplomas, awards and degree ceremonies, accompanied by gowns and mortar boards, start at the age of three; where observable progress in particular subjects is the be-all and end-all of a child's life; where parents make sacrifices to keep their child on the ladder that leads through university to a good job and success.

Sadly, I have seen a similar process at work in Sunday schools and Bible classes, in which pupils are handed sheets of paper with answers that they must tick. At the end of the lesson the papers are collected in and marked. I wonder how this contributes to the growth of love.

This may seem like a jaundiced summary of education, but the purpose is simply to raise our awareness of the underlying philosophy and trends in order to be alert critics of the system. Schools and education, in my view, will undergo a revolution in the next two or three decades due to the impact of new technologies. If so, we can be prepared to be part of this change by examining the roots of what is happening.

Media

In *The Spirit of the Child*, David Hay and Rebecca Nye consider the nature of child spirituality. In the process, they describe what they call the 'social destruction' of spirituality. One of their conclusions is that 'the adult world into which our children are inducted is more often than not destructive to their spirituality'.[5] A significant aspect that we need to consider is the role of the media in contemporary constructions of childhood.

The growing child worldwide is exposed to a huge amount of advertising and marketing through emerging forms of electronic communication, which is often not mediated via parent figures. Is it possible that one effect of this exposure might be to diminish the child's sense of self-worth? What is there to affirm the child's value in God's sight or in the sight of parents and local community? Isn't the prevailing message something to do with possession of the right artefacts—clothes and image being the key to significance and worth?

This marketing is coupled, for the growing child, with the 'cult of celebrity'—'celebrity' meaning someone who is widely recognized through representations on television and other media. The celebrities have a lifestyle that is greatly to be desired, and children as well as adults are invited to share in it in a variety of ways, including books, clothes, photographs and websites, but the ultimate consequence of this process is that the child feels in some way inferior to the celebrity. Life for most people is not a successful attempt to achieve the proffered experiences of happiness, fame and connectedness.[6]

Consumerism

Consumerism goes hand in hand with commodification: things have a monetary value (in fact, that is the primary way of rating them) and in the market people compete to buy or sell them. This is well-tried territory in economics and sociology. Families have been moving, in many parts of the world, from being a unit of production to a unit of consumption, for example. Corporations operating in the global marketplace increasingly target children as consumers. Children consume food and sweets, clothes and especially media products such as DVDs, PlayStations and associated products. Brands and branding are key elements in consumerism. If a child can be won over to a particular brand, this loyalty may last throughout life. Football clubs are brands in this respect.

It does not take a big leap of imagination to see that this process is not conducive to the growth of love. Children are coaxed to see themselves as consumers looking out for products that will please them; they will be insatiable in this search, otherwise advertising has failed. What value does consumerism place on love? What of 'I' and 'thou'? What of giving and creating? What of making and shaping? What do we ultimately mean when we speak of a human being: is he or she a thinker (I think, therefore I am), a maker (*homo faber*), an independent individual (I am self-made), or a child of God (*imago dei*)? If, as humans, we are all to see ourselves primarily as consumers, imagine what long-term damage that might do to the social fabric of families, communities and societies.

A child squeezed into the mould of a consumer is at risk of losing what is meant by childhood. What have consumerism and consumption got to do with spontaneous play, with affection and love? We will realize that they are, in some respects, opposites—if we can get beyond the notion of expressing love by cards and gifts on Valentine's Day and on other special occasions. Love is reciprocal, trusting, faithful, kind, gentle, not boastful and so on. Consumption cannot comprehend love.

The demise of lifelong marriage covenant

If children grow up in a social world where they cannot experience and witness lifelong covenant, this, in my view, is a real handicap in their understanding of the true nature of love.

People have very different experiences of and views about marriage, but even its sternest critics would realize, I think, that children need some real-life examples of covenant love in action—or, if not covenant love, then covenants.[7] Since the 1960s in the West, the idea of lifelong covenant marriage as the basis for family life and the rearing of children has been challenged. I read this week of a professional who said that it was all about choice, and that we (presumably the state and its citizens) should support 'whatever choice people made'.

So if a single unsupported teenage mother decides to have four children by different fathers and spend her life devotedly caring for them, should the state support her? Not in Britain, because the government is seeking to discourage teenage pregnancy—but on what moral grounds, if choice is to be respected? Should the state not support that choice?

This thinking tests the philosophy of liberalism and individualism if it goes no further than the rights of the individual at a point in time. What if there is a housing estate where no one chooses to marry, and all children grow up with a sequence of 'uncles'? What might the situation be like two or three generations down the line? What understanding of covenant and love will there be? What will the children (and adults, for that matter) mean by family and kin?

The social experiment on which we have embarked, based on

cohabitation as a norm, is still to be evaluated, and I am very worried. The households on such estates are likely to become state- and media-dependent, economically and ideologically—not a suitable role model for parenting.

Sexualization

We live in a so-called 'sexual revolution'. The politics of sex have been exposed: the rise of feminism has challenged male domination (where rape has been portrayed by some as the normal form of sexual relationship between a male and a female, within or outside marriage), and the norm of heterosexual sexuality has been challenged. It is not my purpose to pronounce on any or all of these developments, but rather to raise awareness of how they contribute to the background of children's lives and the formation of their sense of sexuality and human relationships.

Childhood is a time of exploration and adventure, some of it sexual, but it is also widely acknowledged that it is a period of latent sexuality, in which identity and cognition are still fluid. The rise of pornography is, in my view, corrosive of adult sexuality and relationships over time, but we have still to realize the potentially devastating effects it may have on the growth of love. Children may get the idea that love is primarily about sexual experimentation and technique—or, even more worrying, that there is no such thing as love, merely sex.

I am not arguing for prudery or a return to a previous age; I am asking that, as 'villagers', we rethink whether we would be prepared to make sacrifices in the interests of our children's emotional and spiritual health and well-being. Jesus was very clear about this matter of sacrifice: he referred to cutting off a hand or taking out an eye, when the welfare of little children was at risk (Mark 9:42–47). We applaud every attempt to protect children from inappropriate touching but, as a society, we have exposed children to images of sexuality without much comment.

A year or two ago, I was interviewed on Radio Two about the views of young people on marriage: a survey had been reported in a magazine called *Bliss*, for teens or 'tweenies'. This was my initiation into the world of teenage magazines for girls. I would guess that most adults are unaware of the content of the media available for children and young people. As villagers, we should be as alert to inappropriate material for children as we are to the dangers that face them on the roads.

The American Psychological Association's Report of 20 February 2007 concluded that inappropriate marketing is leading to the sexualization of children. This marketing involves toys (including Bratz dolls), clothes, magazines, music and the internet, and the negative consequence can be seen in the development of girls. Imposing sexuality on young girls diminishes their cognitive functioning, physical and mental health and healthy sexual development. Negative consequences can include shame and anxiety, eating disorders, low self-esteem, depression and difficulty in establishing a healthy sexual self-image. Sue Palmer, the author of *Toxic Childhood*, comments that mothers who dress their young daughters sexually do not make the connection between their action and something that they are most afraid of—paedophilia.[8]

Fundamentalism

One of the realities of the 21st century that has taken many pundits by surprise is the rise of religious fundamentalism. Sociologists of religion had mistaken the decline of religion in Europe for the norm worldwide. One of the biggest surprises in the UK is the fact that many of the radical Muslims who are prepared to become suicide bombers because of their religious beliefs are from middle-class households that seemed to be integrated into British ways of life and culture.

Much has been written on this subject, so here we will focus on the ways in which fundamentalism affects children and young people. Increasingly, we live in a global village. Even if we do not live side by side with people from different cultures, we are aware of the diversity of the human family through electronic information and travel. The power of the media corporations and the Western dominance of the media are great, and are seen as oppressive to many people in the world.

One of the ways of coping with diversity is to become part of a community that sees the world in terms of black and white, good and bad, and itself as the embodiment of all virtues and the recipient of divine authority. For children caught up in this sort of group or movement, it is difficult, if not impossible, to form the sort of relationships outside their own community that will, in time, constitute a microcosm of the world at large. Faith groups are presented with the challenge of how to nurture the specific faith of their community without demonizing the beliefs of all others.

Multiculturalism

A new challenge is emerging in the UK with the demise of the prevailing consensus on multiculturalism. We once believed that it was possible to construct and maintain civic and civil life on the basis of mutual tolerance, individual freedom and decency in a predominantly secular context. Institutions such as schools would seek to be morally and religiously neutral as far as possible. This approach (which is not the one taken in much of the rest of the world, notably Muslim societies) has not been able to survive the challenges of globalization, reactions to it in religious, cultural and political forms, and the realities of life.

It is one thing to believe that 'mature and educated adults' might be able to live this way (even though they may not have demonstrated the ability to do so in the past) but quite another to believe that children can. Children need firm roots, boundaries and a sense of belonging to a group that has myths, a history and common patterns, festivals, celebrations and rites of passage.

The rituals in the Old Testament were not only inclusive of

children, as we have seen (see Exodus 12: 1–27 on the Passover), but also those from other people groups. In the case of the Passover, the celebration continued and other groups were invited to become fully part of it (vv. 48–49).

One of the most popular institutions in contemporary Britain is the faith school. However much the prevailing liberal ideology condemns them, parents and children seek out these schools keenly. Perhaps parents and children can see beyond mere results, and know that a form of moral community is essential to healthy social relationships.

The risk society

An assumption that the reduction of risk is a primary value is itself a risk to children and childhood. Of course there should be a reasonable awareness of and reduction of risk, but a child needs to explore and, in the process, there will be mistakes, unpleasant discoveries, stings and bumps. A childhood free of all these mishaps would be sterile and would also prevent the development of the crucial ability to make our own risk assessments.

In addition, a risk society tends to operate centrally and bureaucratically, by directives and guidance accompanied by standards and inspections. In the process, the responsibilities of families and children for their own assessments is diminished, and the language of discourse is changed from that of direct experience and observation ('Ow!') to the calculating, reserved language of law and organization.

SUMMARY

In the global village, we are failing our children in part because we have not rigorously questioned prevailing trends and ideologies. We are still trying to fit children and the growth of love into the dominant contemporary discourses, whereas love should be the basis of revised discourses. If we look at the big picture, children are often at risk because they are still invisible or marginal where it really matters.

None of these movements or trends is insuperable over time. Each can be challenged, and we must start by 'lighting candles' in our own homes, schools, churches and communities.

⁓

Chapter Ten

VILLAGES AND
COMPOST HEAPS

But a few seeds did fall on good ground where the plants
produced a hundred or sixty or thirty times as much as was
scattered.

Matthew 13:8

In this final chapter the predominant metaphor changes from that
of hands to those of gardening, farming and the natural world of
plants and vegetation, and 'villages'. I have deliberately not defined
what I mean by 'love' exactly.[1] My sense is that we all have an inbuilt
intuition about what love means, and it is sometimes best to leave
such unspoken assumptions undisturbed.[2] In this book I have used
'love' in an inclusive way: any form of love requires elements of
communication, respect, trust and mutuality. My concern has been
to identify the factors that are likely to nurture the capacity for such
relationships from early childhood and those that are likely to
undermine this capacity.

At this point I would like to draw together some points about
how we can contribute to the environment in which love is most
likely to thrive. I have conceded already, and continue to do so, that
love may thrive in the most unlikely settings—indeed, that in some
ways it seems to thrive on adversity. However, there is much that we
can do to ensure a compost-like soil in which the very first seeds of
love can take root rather than finding themselves swept away or
withering from lack of nourishment.

Among those who read this book there will almost certainly be parents, teachers and leaders of children's work and organizations, who are daily engaged with children. There will also be ministers, grandparents, Christians and professionals who are not so involved, but the underlying message of the book is universal, because we are all part of the 'village' that it takes to parent a child.

So what are the elements of the social compost to which we can contribute? We could respond by restating the five themes, but here the intention is to link them together in order to identify common threads. Using Urie Bronfenbrenner's social typology, drawn from a comparison with ecology, we are thinking about all the levels of the social system of which a child and family are part. The following thoughts stem from the whole argument of the book, with particular reference to the trends and ideologies listed in the previous chapter.

COVENANT

Many years as a sociologist, parent, lecturer and one who is charged with the protection and care of hurting children and young people have combined to convince me that covenant is integral to love. For love to grow, there has to be an idea in the mind of two or more people about what they mean by love, and that idea has to be shared over time.[3] So it is likely that the two or more people (from now on I will refer to two for the sake of brevity) in question will have examples, stories and ideas in their minds that contribute, consciously or unconsciously, to what they mean by love.

Many make the association between love and romance, and in contemporary society this is often reduced to variations on the theme of sexual relationships or sexual activity. Another element in many loving relationships is common interests and commitments—perhaps hobbies like music, cinema, gardening or a sport. It is difficult to think of relationships where there is nothing in common between the partners.

It is my submission that all loving relationships have some shared intimation or intuition of covenant. This involves commitment and loyalty beyond the call of mere interest, self-interest or gratification, calculated benefits or time-limited goals, and one-way giving or receiving. For this idea to be in the mind, there must be examples or stories from which the idea is derived, and so this covenant must exist in literature or in real life for the two people to know about it.

Marriage is one of the most important examples of this covenant in practice. There may be any number of divorces, but it only needs one lasting and loving marriage in the couple's experience to constitute the basis for this idea in their mind. There are surprisingly few other rituals in modern society (compared to feudal systems and tribal groups) where loyalty between members is publicly sworn, and lifelong commitments are pledged to organizations, clubs or communities.[4]

Significantly, the covenant between Christ and his people—sealed with the blood of Jesus, the one who gave his life for his friends—is described as a marriage covenant in the New Testament, and human marriage is seen in Ephesians 6:23–32 as a reflection of this divine love. It is a way of describing or representing the love from which we cannot be separated (Romans 8:38–39). Children who are part of services of Holy Communion will become familiar with this story as it forms a framework for devoted worship by their parents and familiar adults.

Children outside the church and unfamiliar with marriage (we live in a time in the UK when more children are unacquainted with marriage in their personal experience than at any other time in recorded history) need to draw on some of the stories in films. This will give them ideas in the mind, but they may see them as ideals in some way beyond realistic human expectation.

What might this mean in practice for members of the global village entrusted with parenting the next generation? At the very least, it will highlight the importance of making and keeping promises. If children grow up in soil with no experience of promises that are made and kept, how will they acquire the idea of relationships that transcend crises, disagreements and adversity, sickness, health, competing attentions and attractions, old age, weariness and poverty?

False promises are like slugs and poison in the social compost of the young child's early years. Politicians and professional footballers will regularly renege on their manifesto promises or contracts in the light of 'events', but somewhere in the village there must be those who demonstrate genuine covenant.

CELEBRATION

In Chapter Six I expressed my appreciation of the ceiligh as a social event, because it embraces the whole community. All children need to live in a 'village'—in the sense of a setting in which there is a rich diversity of human life—so that they interact with a variety of people, professions, cultures, personalities and so on. A children's village made up only of children will not do; nor will an all-female or all-male environment. A choir school that only has music on its curriculum will not do—and the list could be continued indefinitely.

In modern societies little children will find much that is stratified and segmented, so how and where will children find the 'ceiligh' experience? Some fortunate ones may find it in an actual village; most urban children will not. Nor will children normally find it in schools, day or boarding. This is where the faith community or close-knit organization comes in. If church means anything in the context of its founder's life and teaching, it means a community of people of every type, young and old, who celebrate what it means to live by grace.

Through the course of a year, a child in a loving church fellowship is likely to experience little acts of kindness week by week, to be able to give and receive (don't underestimate how important the collection is in the regular service for children), to sing and dance, to make things, to play and play about, and to be part of the exciting festivals each year, as well as pilgrimages, Christian events, camps and celebrations. Children will see members of this community finding ways of living together, making allowances, working at tasks, respecting one another and contributing to a whole that does not worship or serve itself.

There will be births, deaths, baptisms, weddings, anniversaries, saints' days and so on. All of human life will be lived in some way, and the child will experience much of it directly over time. Where it is a community of the sort that Paul urges in Colossians 3, it is here that children will learn much of what love means in practice.

SPIRITUALITY

Some readers may be wondering if and when we will get down to the serious business of discussing, exploring and celebrating the growth of love between a child and God. By this we mean, of course, both the receiving of love and the giving of love in response. Why wasn't spirituality included among the five main themes of this book, for example?

I confess that one of the reasons I write little about spirituality is that I don't feel that it is conducive to being put into words in a book of prose. To me, silence, music, colours and poetry offer a better vehicle. An equally fundamental point, however, is that we have been considering how love grows in all its manifestations and varieties. We have not been trying to restrict our field of vision to the way love grows between parents and children, between peers, between people of a common faith, or between people of different faiths. As love grows, it expresses itself in giving and receiving in a wider circle until 'all in the end is love'. The 'I/thou' relationship that is a cornerstone of genuine love can exist between all people, and between people and God.

In drawing from the scriptures, we acknowledge how God has revealed to us what love is, through the creation, his actions, prophets, people and, uniquely, Jesus. 'Real love isn't our love for God, but his love for us. God sent his Son to be the sacrifice by which our sins are forgiven' (1 John 4:10). Theologically speaking, all that we have considered is set within the ultimate context of God's love for us. This is the source of love: 'since God loved us this much, we must love each other' (v. 11). So God is not simply another object or person whom we may love and who loves us. He is the ground of love, the source of love, the context of love and the medium of love.

Children in families, as they learn to accept love from a parent, are not just preparing themselves for the possibility of loving God and receiving him one day. Whether or not they are conscious of it, they are being loved by him through their parents; in responding in love, they also love God. There is a rich theme in the teaching of Jesus about this, which continues the teaching of the prophets.

Some years ago, we were having our daily reading for adults at Mill Grove and there was a comment in the Scripture Union notes to this effect: 'Our love for God is no greater than our love for the person we least like.' I instinctively rebelled: this was unthinkable and impossible. In that case, I thought, my love for God is abominably weak and poor—and try as I might, over the years, I have not been able to wriggle out of the essential truth of this proposition.

James, in typically down-to-earth language, summarizes what he sees as the core of the teaching of the scriptures about relating to God (translated as 'religion'): 'Religion that pleases God the Father must be pure and spotless. You must help needy orphans and widows and not let this world make you evil' (James 1:27).

In the teaching of Jesus we find that receiving (an important and strong word) children is identified with receiving Jesus and God: 'When you welcome even a child because of me, you welcome me. And when you welcome me, you welcome the one who sent me' (Mark 9:37). In the parable of the sheep and goats, both sheep and goats are mystified about the fact that they cared for and failed to care for the king, respectively. 'Lord, when did we see you...?' they both ask, and the reply is, 'Whatever you did (not do) for one of the least of these brothers of mind, you did (not do) for me' (Matthew 25:37–45, NIV).

There is no doubt in the mind of the writers of these passages that God is God and his creatures are his creatures: there is no pantheism here at all. But God has come close in human beings; those whom he created in his image.

Loving God by means of specialist religious activities such as prayer, offerings or festivals can never be a substitute for right relationships between human beings: 'When you spread out your hands in prayer, I will hide my eyes from you; even if you offer many prayers, I will not listen. Your hands are full of blood... Seek justice, encourage the oppressed. Defend the cause of the fatherless' (Isaiah 1:15, 17, NIV: note the symbol of hands used here).

The general point of this chapter is that if we are seeking to encourage children to accept and respond to God's love, we will do it not by teaching them specifically religious symbols, language, patterns and methods; we will not do it by encouraging precocious development in forms of meditative or contemplative prayer. There is no separate realm in which a different form of love and loving is to be learned. Love grows on earth among human beings thanks to God's grace and love, which enfolds and inspires all love.

Over time, we will teach children specific things about the scriptures, our faith, theology, worship and so on, but that teaching is not about the growth of love. Love comes before these things and will, in time, express itself in these ways as in others. Let us assume that children grow up in a household where grace is said before meals, where church attendance is regular, where prayers are said kneeling at the foot of the bed each evening, where tithing is the norm, and where reading the Bible together at the meal table is a habit. What relationship does all this have to the growth of love? It is possible that through such activities children will learn the security of a patterned life and boundaries, and they may be moved by the stories from the Bible, but it is the way the activities are done—the examples set by the parents, the way the parents internalize the meaning of prayer and Bible reading—that is most important. Are the daily lives of the parents consistent with what the children are being taught?

THE COMMON THINGS OF LIFE

In the light of all this, how can we live in a way that will encourage love to grow? It will be the little things that make a difference—the daily round and common task; the regular encounters, greetings and farewells; shared experiences; our response to animals and the natural world, to music, art and literature, as well as our life together as 'church'. Love will grow in and through countless unremembered acts of kindness.

That is where and why all villagers have a part to play: every encounter and every event matters in some way. Little children (as Montessori stated and we should all notice) are absorbent: they drink in and digest what is going on around them at a deep level. It forms the raw material on which they base their responses to situations (trust or distrust, and so on). As I have observed before, children often recall a single event as if it happened regularly, so the stakes are high.

All the hidden little acts of kindness combine to make up the social soil in which love grows. Those who have thought much about the spirituality of children talk in terms of relatedness and connectedness, and we are thinking here, in essence, about the same process in some shape or form. Love is about relatedness and, as it grows, there is the potential for it to connect all things together.

Church comprises both the 'little family' of the child's household and the bigger family of the local fellowship of Christians. In both of these communities and through the relationships between them, whatever children are learning about love will find associations with the story of God's nature and, specifically, his love.

'Love has its reasons that reason itself cannot fathom,' wrote French philosopher Blaise Pascal, and it is from the base and experience of love that love is known. It is the relationships of significant others that break into a child's life, representing, evoking and modelling this love. As love is experienced, it grows: 'I pray that you, being rooted and established in love, may have power, together with all the saints, to grasp how wide and long and high and deep is the love of Christ, and to know this love that surpasses knowledge —that you may be filled to the measure of all the fullness of God' (Ephesians 3:17–19, NIV).

HEALTHY PATTERNS OF LIFE

People have tried many different teaching methods and models of community to help children grow and develop physically, socially, cognitively and spiritually. They may not use the word 'love', but let us give them the benefit of the doubt and assume that this is what they have in the back of their minds. What is the very best model for us to copy and live out?

I will not try to list the villages, communes, soviets, kibbutzim, ranches, residential schools and methods of parenting that have been tried, but there is one overall comment to which I return: the village is a good model to have in mind as a template. By now, I trust you realize that I am not thinking simply of a rural community, and especially not some attempt to recall the mythical golden era of communities and families. What I am trying to describe is a place or setting in which a child experiences healthy patterns of life, each day, each week, each month, each year and through the stages of life.

Rather than looking to one method or a group of specialists on whom the whole burden falls of creating the social soil for the growth of love, I am thinking of a multi-faceted, interwoven set of relationships, connections and links. Over time, in such a context, a child will learn how to relate to, cope with and reciprocate what we know as love. In such a setting, there will be space that is private to the child and to his or her family (however small and cramped) and links with other families in a safe setting. There will be the opportunity for a child to play with peers, to observe and help adults in a variety of forms of household, community and productive tasks. There will be sensitive adult encouragement and instruction to relate to the world of nature, including the night sky and the seasons, starting with tiny grubs, leaves and petals, spiders' webs and frosted blades of grass. There will be yearly festivals, each marking out the child's year and offering a framework within which to relate to and understand some of the features of the universe into which the child has been born.

Rites of passage will be a natural part of this village, and the villagers will take part in them together: conception, birth, baptism, naming or dedication, the start of school, puberty, leaving school, starting at college, work or apprenticeship, marriage, parenthood, death—and festivals like Easter and the Ascension, which look beyond death. Much of this process will be prefigured, modelled and represented in the world of nature, with, for example, the birth, life and death of animals and the differences between the seasons.

I hope you can see that where a child is part of a family and community that encounter and celebrate all of this together, we find the social compost in which love can grow. We are not looking for the ideal community, but for that which is 'good enough'.

FORMING NEW COMMUNITIES

How can we find or form and nurture such communities where they do not already exist? I think this may be the greatest political, social and practical challenge for all who make the growth of love their priority, for I am not sure that there is any alternative. In urban areas, it might be possible to think again about radical ideas such as the discarded Scottish proposal for community councils, where local people decided the boundaries of the area of which they felt a part.[5] I am not sure, however, that such an area or council could be created on the basis of place (that is, where people share a common area of land on which they live). Electronic technology and emerging senses of identity have rendered such notions largely redundant for the time being, but I would not rule them out for future times, when there may be extreme threats or stress, and people are forced to work together for their very survival.

Schools are an obvious candidate for such communities: the idea of extended schools in the UK resonates with this thinking and the best are, indeed, like little villages. Again, though, the regulations, bureaucracy and institutionalization of schools in the world are against it.

Try as we might, I think we are driven back to faith communities (and by this I am happy to go way beyond the traditional definition of faith and religion) as the most likely source of the 'village' (apart from rural areas where a village of sorts exists already). Taking my life at Mill Grove as a constant reminder that it can be done, I would suggest that it is not just formal churches that can fulfil this function but extended families or households. These are common in many parts of the world, where a child is part of a system or network of communications and interlocking sets of relationships, which make up some sort of coherent local community with a healthy pattern of life, linking personal experiences and life stages with the celebration of the movement of the years and the planets.

If I look back at where I have seen love grow in the community of Mill Grove, I would think of the death of pets, and some of us gathering around in the orchard where they were buried; funerals where children were present; festivals and celebrations where we have joined with what is happening nationally (Remembrance or bonfire night) or worldwide (Easter and Christmas); birthdays, mealtimes, illness, accidents, bedtimes, holidays and the like. Over time and in time, a child will thus experience a growing number of events and situations in a social context and learn how to respond to them.

All this, like compost, is not very glamorous but it does reflect the wisdom of the ages and different cultures. Such villages are extremely hard to create and very easy to undermine and destroy. But we must try to create them, for it takes a village to parent—and by that I mean not only the villagers but also the setting in which they can relate to each other predictably and comfortably. In saying this, I do not intend in any way to undermine or undervalue the role of the nuclear family, with mother and father married to each other: I have stressed the importance of the marriage covenant. But this nuclear family is fragile if not connected with the 'village' through extended family and numerous social links and bonds. It cannot be seen to exist in its own right as a sort of castle separated from the rest of the social world by a metaphorical wall and moat.

THINKING GLOBALLY

While writing this book, I have tried to keep in mind a range of children. They include those from 'good enough' families, those who experience the separation of their parents and a disturbed family life, those from peaceful countries and those from war-ravaged zones, those who are healthy and those whose families and communities have been ravaged by disease, those who are wealthy and those who are poor, isolated families where a single mother and child live in a flat, extended families where cousins regularly see each other, and so on.

When teaching, I have tried as often as possible to stay with families and listen to the stories of children, families and communities. The places have included England, Scotland, Wales and Ireland, France, Belgium, the Netherlands, Germany, Austria and Switzerland, the Czech Republic, Greece, Israel, Serbia, Russia, Malaysia, Singapore, India, Thailand, Nepal, Sri Lanka, Australia, Brazil, Ecuador, America, Canada and the Caribbean.

Everything I have written in each chapter is intended to connect with the realities of each setting and culture. What makes for good social compost seems to apply universally: covenant, celebration, spirituality and healthy patterns of life are important and practicable worldwide.

There will be specialist responses to the needs of some children because of their traumas and particular gifts or needs, but, however damaged and needy they may be, the village remains relevant—possibly even more relevant. A school may be an overwhelming place for many children but a village is different because it can cope with extraverts and introverts, those who thrive on the limelight and public space, and those who crave privacy and anonymity.

CONCLUSION

It has been my joy and privilege to see evidence of human love growing in every climate and every situation in which I have found myself, however unlikely. I do not understand how and why love grows as and where it does—in fact, I marvel more and more that it does—but my hunch is that in the mind of the child who begins to receive and reciprocate this love, there is a village in some shape or form—embryonic or more mature.

We do not have to wait for utopian conditions, IMF funding, religious revivals and the like; we can and must start where we are. We can live as villagers in twos and threes in streets, blocks of flats, churches and estates. A government plan for uniform villages in a region or nation would be a disaster. We cannot wait for experts to produce blueprints, because they will see the world through their specialisms and villages, by their nature, resist such things.

Compost heaps are among the most common yet complex entities on earth, where hundreds of identifiable systems and communities live in connection with each other, seasoned by the sunlight, rain and natural environment of the whole. I suggest that the compost heap is a sensible analogy for a village. We cannot plan either of them in detail: we create the conditions, put relevant materials on to the heap, and leave the rest to happen. The outcome isn't surprising, but it is almost impossible to predict the exact processes by which it has been produced. If we try to control the processes by means of separation and pesticides, we will destroy the compost heap.

It sounds precarious and messy, but that is the reality. Without some form of compost, the earth could not survive as we know it, and without the social life of villages as we have conceived them, human civilization as we know it could not survive. Furthermore, somewhere deep within the village, love is being nurtured in myriad unseen ways.

As I come to the end of this book, I realize that it has been my privilege to live in just such a village. It is imperfect, frustrating, mixed, largely unknown and unrecognized, but it is a place where love has grown—love expressed for spouses, children, families and community, for nature, nations, the world and for God whom we dare to call our heavenly Father.

NOTES

Introduction

1   Readers acquainted with my published work may recognize echoes of previous material. A chapter of the *Barclay Report* was based on this thinking ('Social Workers: Their Roles and Tasks', NISW, 1982, pp. 64–65). There was also an article in the journal *Social Work Today* Vol. 14, No. 38, 14 June 1983. More recently, there has been a chapter in *Celebrating Children* (G. Miles and J-J. Wright, eds., Paternoster, 2003, pp. 123–126). In addition, students around the world have heard me speak on the subject of 'A five-fingered exercise on a four-letter word' as part of the Master's course on Holistic Child Development.

2   Frank Lake, *Clinical Theology*, DLT, 1986.

3   Bruce Reed, *The Dynamics of Religion*, DLT, 1978.

4   James E. Loder, *The Logic of the Spirit: Human Development in Theological Perspective*, Jossey Bass, 1998.

5   Paul Tournier, *The Meaning of Persons*, SCM, 1957.

6   Paul Tournier, *A Place for You*, SCM, 1968.

7   R.S. Lee, *Freud and Christianity*, Penguin, 1967.

8   Victor Frankl, *Man's Search for Meaning*, Hodder, 1962.

9   Carl Jung, *Modern Man in Search of a Soul*, RKP, 1961.

10   Roger Hurding, *Roots and Shoots*, Hodder, 1985.

11   There are several papers on the Child Theology Movement's website, where this and other connections are explored (www.childtheology.org).

12   Hillary Clinton, *It Takes a Village*, Touchstone, 1996.

13   John Bowlby, *Maternal Care and Mental Health*, WHO, 1952.

14   John Bowlby, *Child Care and the Growth of Love*, Penguin, 1953.

15   Ibid., p. 78.

16   Ibid., p. 13.

17   Ibid., p. 37.

Chapter One: The place where we started

1 The story has been charted in various books about the place, including Bob Holman, 'Not Like Any Other Home', Campaign Literature, 1994.

2 For those who recall the work of George Müller and Hudson Taylor, there is a close link with their understanding of 'works of faith'.

3 This means that it is possible to receive children into our care without undue bureaucracy and procedures.

4 See, for example, S. Murray and A. Wilkinson-Hayes, Hope from the Margins: New Ways of Being Church, Grove Books, 2000.

5 Examples include the many varieties of religious orders, Iona, Taizé, L'Arche, S.O.S. Kinderdorff, Pestalozzi, Christian communes, the Bruderhof, Mukti and types of foster family. The writers include Benedict, Dietrich Bonhoeffer, Barbara Dockar-Drysdale, Jean Vanier and many others.

6 If you are interested in further reflections on this, there is an article in Crucible, July–September 2005, pp. 24–30. Individuals, as well as professional and legal institutions, have norms or stereotypes in their minds when describing or categorizing groups, and labels are assigned because it is impossible to live without them. As Zygmunt Bauman has pointed out in much of his recent writing, anything that seems ambivalent or un-usual is unsettling and disturbing (see for example, Modernity and Ambivalence, Polity, 1993).

7 When social workers talk of 'prevention' they mean among other things keeping children out of residential care.

8 In this respect I have much in common with Stuart T. Hauser, Joseph P. Allen and Eve Golden, authors of Out of the Woods: Tales of Resilient Teens, Harvard University Press, 2006. Writing about children who had been incarcerated in a mental asylum, they conclude that, astonishingly, a handful are thriving 20 years on. They have formed lasting friendships and are

responsible and loving parents. It would be possible to focus on those who have not made it, but the fact is that some have not only survived but thrived.

9   This description comes from W.H. Vanstone, *Love's Endeavour, Love's Expense: The Response of Being to the Love of God*, DLT, 1977.

10 Robert Frost, 'Mending Wall', in *North of Boston*, David Nutt, 1914.

11 In fact, my grandmother did not feel that her life's work was complete until I had assured her that I would continue to pray for one of the older boys, a journalist, with whom we had all lost contact. She had prayed for him without fail every day, and I promised that I would take over. She died very soon after I gave her this assurance.

12 One of the groups that might seem relatively unimportant is a badminton club that functions every Friday evening during the winter season. It has been going since 1947. Here, generations of children have had the chance to play with neighbours and friends from local churches: for them, it is an introduction to the world of voluntary groups and sporting associations.

13 *Links* is sent each Easter to everyone who is in some way connected with the family of Mill Grove.

14 There are writers who try to establish a model of a 'biblical family'. My 20 years of working on a complete new edition of the Bible have constantly reminded me of the great variety of family arrangements in the scriptures, and how flawed and tortuous the relationships in them were.

Chapter Two: Five-finger exercise on a four-letter word

1   UN Convention on the Rights of the Child, adopted by the General Assembly 20 November 1989.

2   Jo-Joy has worked on this issue with me in *Celebrating Children*, ch. 16, and in subsequent conversations and joint teaching.

3 Jo-Joy Wright, unpublished paper presented to the *Celebrating Children* course held at Mill Grove in February 2006.

4 John Bowlby specifically noted 'poor concentration at school': *Child Care*, p. 37.

5 Charlotte Towle, *Common Human Needs*, Allen and Unwin, 1945 (out of print).

6 Mia Kellmer Pringle, *The Needs of Children*, Hutchinson, 1974 (out of print).

7 T.B. Brazelton and S.I. Greenspan, *The Irreducible Needs of Children*, Perseus Publishing, 2000.

8 In my typology, a) is security, b), c) and d) are significance, e) is creativity, f) boundaries and g) community.

9 'Resilience' is a difficult term; we shall return to it later.

10 I am grateful to Kathryn Copsey for summarizing these concepts in her book and in conversation. Berne's list includes recognition hunger, contact hunger, stimulus hunger, structure hunger and sexual hunger. Kathryn Copsey, *From the Ground Up*, BRF, 2005, pp. 39–52.

11 A classic and possibly controversial example is James Fowler, *Stages of Faith*, Harper, 1995.

12 David Hay and Rebecca Nye, *The Spirit of the Child*, Fount, 1998.

13 If so, that is the way integration often begins: thesis, antithesis and then synthesis, if we take the Hegelian approach.

14 Loder, op.cit. My friend and colleague Jerome Berryman has told me how influential another book by Loder has been in his own thinking and work: *The Transforming Moment*, Harper-Collins, 1981.

15 Human development is shown most frequently in terms of steps, stages, or a pyramid. Loder's diagram shows it as a circle that goes nowhere in theological terms! It is not development at all, seen in this wider context.

16 Loder, op. cit., p. 74.

17 See, for example, Jean Piaget, *The Language and Thought of the Child*, Harcourt Brace, 1926.

18 'The conversion of Northumbria', from Bede's *Ecclesiastical History*, in Sweet's *Anglo-Saxon Primer* ed. N. Davis, OUP, 1955, pp. 90–91.

19 Frances Young, *Face to Face: A Narrative Essay in the Theology of Suffering*, Continuum, 1990.

20 Caroline Philps, *Elizabeth Joy: A Mother's Story*, Lion Hudson, 1984.

21 Henri Nouwen, *Adam: God's Beloved*, DLT, 1997.

22 I find T.S. Eliot's *Four Quartets* to be one of the deepest explorations of this relationship (Faber, 1944).

23 Loder labels this 'developmental egocentrism' (op. cit., p. 76).

24 If we are looking for an analogy of the relationship between common models of child development and a theological perspective, Loder provides it via Karl Barth and a paper by Barth's Scottish follower and exponent, Professor T.F. Torrance. The paper argues that in the realm of geometry everything proceeded on Euclidean lines alongside, and distinct from, physics. Space was the uncriticized assumption of this geometrical understanding or description of the 'world'. This was before relativity, before Einstein. Now the whole relationship between space (that is, geometry) and time and speed has been reconceptualized by contemporary understandings of physics. Loder (following Barth and Torrance) is calling for a similar revolution in the social sciences. (In some ways, this has been taking place under the guise of the collapse of modernity and the emergence of 'post-modernity', but this description does not adequately reveal what Loder is seeking to describe.) T.F. Torrance, 'The Natural Theology of Karl Barth', quoted in Loder, op. cit., pp. 32–33.

25 Indecisive because it does not deal with the ultimate questions of the meaning of life and death.

26 *Kairos* is a time when something special happens, as when the eternal intersects with the everyday; *chronos* is sequential, quantitative time.

27 There is an excellent section on this subject entitled 'Here-and-Now' in Hay and Nye, op. cit., pp. 60–63.

28 If readers are reeling at this point, it may help to say that just as the study of geometry goes on and the Euclidean framework continues to work for much of what we can observe, so a lot of child development theory makes basic sense in educational and social work. What I am doing is to relocate this whole theory in such a way that theology, far from being a separate field of study, or an add-on at Sunday school, becomes part of the revised paradigm. It will not do for theology to become a junior partner in the conversation. Starting from the facts of pre-birth, death, the search for meaning and the fear of nothingness (which, we may guess, lies at the heart of Richard Dawkins' 'evangelical' fervour, like that of much religion, political and cultural life), theology challenges the cosiness of much development theory and perhaps the institutional status quo that legitimates traditional and current educational theory and methods. Thomas Kuhn would call it a 'prevailing paradigm' (Thomas Kuhn, *The Structure of Scientific Revolutions*, University of Chicago Press, 1962).

29 Kurt's wife, Pamela Pick, wrote a book, which I had the privilege of editing, that demonstrated how keenly they both saw into my experience at Mill Grove. They too lived in a residential community. The book is called *Tree Tops: An Example of Creative Residential Care*, RCA, 1981.

30 One of the best books I know on this process is Vanstone's *Love's Endeavour, Love's Expense*.

31 S. Hample and E. Marshall, eds., *Children's Letters to God*, Kylie Kathie, 1992.

Chapter Three: Security

1 Other words included in the meaning are survival, safety and protection.

2 For precisely this reason, Camilla Batmanghelidjh calls her book, describing the harsh realities of the lives of children, *Shattered Lives* (Kids Company, 2006).

3 Like Bruce Reed, I believe that this is one of the most perfectly constructed and ordered of all Christian services.

4 Dan Hughes, *Building the Bonds of Attachment: Awakening Love in Deeply Troubled Children*, Rowman and Littlefield, 2004.

5 D.W. Winnicott writes, 'The first ego organisation comes from the experience of threats of annihilation which do not lead to annihilation and from which, repeatedly, there is recovery' 'Primary Maternal Preoccupation', in *Through Paediatrics to Psycho-Analysis*, Basic Books, 1975.

6 John Bowlby, *A Secure Base: Clinical Applications of Attachment Theory*, Routledge, 1988.

7 Ibid., p. 4.

8 Ibid., p. 11.

9 I am deliberately linking D.W. Winnicott's idea to Bowlby's description of security here.

10 Rowan Williams, *Lost Icons*, T&T Clark, 2000 (Chapter One, 'Childhood and Choice').

11 Bruce Reed makes this the framework for his seminal work, *The Dynamics of Religion*. He argues that it is one of the primary functions of orthodox religion to provide a setting in which this process of oscillation between extra dependence (that is, the voyage) and intra dependence (that is, time in the harbour) is regulated and managed (p. 52). In conversation, Bruce used to tell me that he wished he had given the book the title *Dynamics of Life*, because the process occurs in every human being, institution and society, religious or secular.

12 It is also a significant challenge to Maslow's simplistic hierarchy of needs, for unless there is some sense of self-actualization (self-esteem built on a secure base) there will not be the desire to address other issues and respond to other 'needs'.

13 Emma K. Adam, 'Beyond Quality: Parental and Residential

Stability and Children's Adjustment' in *Current Directions in Psychological Science*, Vol. 13, No. 5, pp. 210–213.

14 One of Winnicott's lasting contributions to our understanding of the developing psyche of the child is his focus on the space between child and real mother (or mother substitute). The 'holding environment' is both psychic and physical. It is this that makes possible a sense of the child's being. Without it the child has not really come into existence and there can be no 'continuity of being' (what we might call identity, or self-worth). For a good selection from D.W. Winnicott's writings, see www.mythosandlogos.com/Winnicott.

15 The Scottish Institute of Residential Child Care finds that it is fighting a never-ending battle to get the voices of children and young people amplified to the point where professionals and professional institutions listen enough to change attitudes and policies.

16 G. Wolff Pritchard, *Offering the Gospel to Children*, Cowley, 1992, p. 43.

17 Bruce Reed writes, 'It is significant that every form of attachment behaviour, and of the behaviour of the attachment-figure, identified by Bowlby, has its close counterpart in the images of the relationship between Israel (or the worshipper) and God which we find in, for example, the Psalms' (op. cit., p. 14).

18 J. Wesley Bready, *Doctor Barnardo*, Allen and Unwin, 1930, p. 74.

Chapter Four: Boundaries

1 One of the best summaries of the role and significance of boundaries in the lives of children is found in Lessons 8 and 9 in Dr Phyllis Kilbourn's *Offering Healing and Hope for Children in Crisis*, Crisis Care International Training, pp. 63–76. The relevant sections are Lesson 8, 'Setting boundaries', and Lesson 9, 'Stop sign model'. See www.rainbowsofhope.org. The idea of 'structure'

is one that provides many practical analogies (for example, with architecture, music, literature, the body and so on).

2 A consequence of such panic and fear is a search for security in other places and ways. My feeling in the case of these two children (now young adults who are both in full-time employment) is that their experience of loss was so deep that they came to rely on Mill Grove as the nearest thing to a substitute womb. It was as if they had to start their emotional life all over again. This is never easy, not least because everything is out of synchronization: their chronological and school ages were completely out of kilter with their emotional development, for example.

3 The traditional Chinese shoes for women are an example of over-restrictive physical boundaries that actually crippled some women.

4 I am thinking here of the work of Basil Bernstein on restricted and unrestricted codes of different social groups.

5 Hughes, *Building the Bonds of Attachment*, pp. 19–23.

6 A useful selection of Janusz Korczak's writings is to be found in ed. Sandra Joseph, *A Voice for the Child*, Thorsons, 1999, pp. 23, 29.

7 Others who have helped me in this discovery include notably Bettelheim, Velazco and the Opies.

8 This is one of the risks of continuous television watching: it provides what may seem like a random collection of images with no overarching story or theme, and little time for or encouragement of reflection.

9 A vivid description of his life and work is to be found in Baroness von Marenholz-Bulow, *Reminiscences of Friedrich Fröbel*, Lee and Shepherd, 1882.

10 My doctoral research in India led me to see how Pandita Ramabai had embodied much of Fröbel's method and philosophy in the residential community she founded, called Mukti.

11 Loder, op. cit., pp. 89–95 is superb on this subject.

12 This is true whether or not the child recognizes or expresses it consciously.

13 This may be an increasing problem in our time when declarations of rights and statements of practice are common. These statements may seem disconnected in the eyes of children from their immediate environment and relationships.

14 I am acutely aware of the way Christians of different denominations have had their childhoods ruined by the fear engendered by such a concept of boundaries: Catholics who feared they had been guilty of a mortal sin; Evangelicals who feared they had committed a sin against the Holy Spirit; Brethren who feared they would be excommunicated from their family because of outside friendships or 'inappropriate' contact with the outside world.

15 The received wisdom at that time (1950 and pre-Bowlby) was that the child should not be told about the impending separation, and there was no provision for the parent to stay with the child.

16 In Chapter Two, I described the world of the child in such a way that family and household were understood as 'kingdom'. School is, for most children, another kingdom, and the process of movement from one to the other is critically important (for that matter, so is the transfer from junior to secondary school). We dare not let adult assumptions dominate the reading of the event: it is an exodus from the known, safe, accepting world of family, into a whole new realm. It is crossing a Rubicon, and marks the end of an old dispensation and entry into the new.

17 There are huge differences around the world and they are, among other things, a sharp and timely reminder of the very big distinction between the life of the boy-child and the girl-child around the world. Even though I do not develop the important theme of gender in this book, I would not want readers to think that the children of whom I write are sexless and that gender is of little relevance.

18 This is one of the main elements of the story that children consider, and it is profoundly disturbing to them.

19 K. Herzog, *Children and Our Global Future*, Pilgrim Press, 2005, p. 46.

20 See Jerome Berryman, *The Complete Guide to Godly Play*, Living the Good News, 2002.

21 Herzog is clear where she stands on this: 'Our search for truth should be anchored in a strong communal tradition that is nevertheless open to constant communication with people of other faiths and cultures to whom we give and from whom we receive' (Herzog, op. cit., p. 52).

Chapter Five: Significance

1 E. Erikson, *Childhood and Society*, Paladin, 1977, p. 30.

2 Ibid., p. 22.

3 P. and B. Berger, *Sociology: A Biographical Approach*, Penguin, 1972, p. 69.

4 Erikson writes that the sense of significance (ego identity) 'depends, I think, on the recognition that there is an inner population of remembered and anticipated sensations and images which are firmly correlated with the outer population of familiar and predictable things and people' (op. cit., p. 222).

5 G.H. Mead, *Mind, Self and Society*, University of Chicago Press, 1934.

6 This was explored memorably by R.D. Laing in relation to the ontology of schizophrenia in *The Divided Self*, Penguin, 1965, and more generally in *Self and Others*, Penguin, 1969. Erikson also saw infantile schizophrenia as one of the clearest results of the absence of basic trust (op. cit., p. 223).

7 An unforgettable example of someone who remained alongside the children in his care to the end is Janusz Korczak. On 6 August 1942, of his own free will, he boarded a train with 200

Jewish orphans to die with them in the gas chambers of Treblinka. This was unconditional commitment.

8   See, for example, 'In Residence' columns in the electronic magazine www.childrenwebmag.com

9   See, for example, Keith J. White, 'Bullying: why it must be tackled in schools' in *Redbridge Children's Network*, March 2007, Issue 12, p. 15.

10 One of those who share exactly this view of life stories is Paul Tournier. In *A Place for You* he writes, 'In order to understand a man [sic] we must follow him into all the detailed places of his life as he describes them to us. We must relive in them with him... That is why it is so important for husband and wife each to visit the places where the childhood of the other has been spent' (p. 16).

11 We are once again recollecting the reflection in Chapter Two about the child's 'kingdom'.

12 Tim Radford, *Guardian* 6 January 2007, Review, p. 10, in a review of Paul Davies, *The Goldilocks Enigma: Why is the Universe Just Right for Life?* Allen Lane, 2006.

13 Ramabai had the ability to identify and empathize with each girl because of her own story of loss and orphanhood, and her encyclopedic knowledge of India from having walked something like 5000 miles throughout its vast and varied towns and villages.

14 Joey Velasco, *They Have Jesus*, Kenosis Publications, 2006.

15 I am not talking, of course, about a child giving details of their life as on a form, but the sharing that is more typical of those in love, over time, and spontaneously.

16 I think that Erik Erikson's great work *Childhood and Society*, with its famous 'eight ages of man' (sic), is based on the notion that in healthy families and childhoods the parent holds the child continuously in mind. The polarities 'trust and mistrust', 'autonomy and shame/doubt' can be resolved where the commitment of the parent is not in any doubt.

17 Martin Buber, *I and Thou*, trans. Ronald Gregor Smith, Charles Scribner's Sons, 1958.
18 Erikson, op. cit., p. 225.
19 Erikson sees one of the most important tasks of parenting as 'to represent to the child a deep, an almost somatic conviction that there is a meaning to what they are doing' (op. cit., p. 224).
20 For a summary of this view see, for example, the Introduction in Marcia Bunge (ed.), *The Child in Christian Thought and Practice*, Eerdmans, 2001.
21 Erikson, op. cit., p. 224.

Chapter Six: Community

1 We note as a matter of fact that there are some children who shun such relationships and become adult recluses, such as Paul Getty, the pianist Glenn Gould and the chess player Bobby Fisher.
2 One key developmental stage that is particularly relevant to the growth of love and to social relationships concerns the age at which little children are able to cope with groups and relationships outside their nuclear families. Research shows that children are not normally prepared for such settings before the age of three years, except in exceptional circumstances.
3 Mary Douglas, the social anthropologist who died in May 2007, famously described humans as 'ritual creatures', and I agree with her perspective on this.
4 For the record, I am thinking of Khedgaon, a village 40 miles east of Pune in western India.
5 In such cases, children may find school deeply problematic because they lack the basic equipment to understand and cope with what is going on in the world of human relationships. It is also true, however, of the rest of life: friends, neighbours and social interaction in general.

6 Article 28 (a): 'Make primary education compulsory and available free to all.'

7 It has been observed that in Uganda the bonding between child and mother continues for about four years in the most continuous and intimate ways: rarely do clothes or material come between the body of the child and her mother. But Pearce noticed that at the age of about four there is a sudden and planned 'abandonment' of the child by the mother. The child, in desperation, seeks something or someone to cling to and finds the tribe and its culture there as a surrogate mother or solution to the crisis. I am not sure how accurate this analysis is or how common it might be in different cultures (see Loder, op. cit., p. 87). Sadly, it is exactly this process that so often lies at the heart of the enlistment of child soldiers. Having been ordered to murder their mother and father, they are left with no one: they are alone in the world. The company of soldiers, in its twisted and horrible way, then provides exactly what the children are looking for, psychologically and emotionally. They have a ready-made surrogate community.

8 This search for community is about belonging to a group in a very committed way, rather like the 'hearth-companions' in Anglo-Saxon times who swore that they would die for one another if necessary. The community is based on a commitment to the whole that is greater than self-interest. We may need here to use the important distinction given to us by the German sociologist Ferdinand Tönnies between *Gemeinschaft* and *Gesellschaft*. The former is about primary communities and belonging, the latter about a secondary form of association.

9 '*Volk*' is a German word which Hitler used to mean 'our people' as distinct from other tribes or nations.

10 The sociologists are worried. See Keith J. White, 'The Social Significance of Marriage' in 1992 *Annual Review* of St George's House, Windsor Castle, pp. 50–67.

11 See Keith J. White, 'Child-friendly space', on Shaftesbury and his wife beside the sea, in *Outlook*, 12 September 2001, p. 11.

12 For example, *Reception Class*, written with Prof. Haddon Willmer and due to be published by SPCK; *An Introduction to Child Theology*, written with Prof. Haddon Willmer, Child Theology Network, 2006.

13 Stanley J. Grenz, *Theology for the Community of God*, Eerdmans, 1994, ch. 7.

14 David Sims has written an unpublished PhD thesis on the effect of affluence on American Evangelical children (Durham University, 2006). There was also a theological experiment on affluence at the 2007 Child Theology consultation in Quito, Ecuador. See also the film, *Bowling for Colombine*, and Robert Putnam, *Bowling Alone: The Collapse and Revival of American Community*, Simon and Schuster, 2000.

15 See Keith J. White, 'What shall we do with 24 million orphans?' www.childrenwebmag.com

16 A student interrupted one of my lectures on world poverty, saying that I was wrong to imply that poor communities were to be pitied. Yes, poverty was a social blight and not to be excused but the communities in which he had grown up in Latin America knew a lot of joy, festivity and belonging.

Chapter Seven: Creativity

1 K. Herzog, *Children and our Global Future*, Pilgrim, 2005, p. 101.

2 D.W. Winnicott, 'Playing: its theoretical status in the clinical situation', *The International Journal of Psychoanalysis* 1968, Volume 49, pp. 591–599.

3 I recall learning Latin in a very traditional way. It began with the first declension—'*Amo, amas, amat, amamus, amatis, amant*'—and continued declension after declension, conjugation after conjugation.

4 We have noted already that universal schooling developed alongside industrialization—so we have factories for adults and schools for children, and both use the language of work and output. Classes used to be laid out in lines and rows, similar to a production line. 'Hothouses' and 'production lines' were the two images that John Westerhoff used at a conference in Chicago in 2006.

5 I was once asked by an inspector in our preschool nursery what I thought a child was learning by using a particular piece of play equipment. I ventured that I had no idea, but that the child seemed to be enjoying himself. I was left in no doubt that I had given the wrong answer for the purposes of the inspection. I should have said something about motor coordination, of course. The idea that play for play's sake is sufficient was not entertained, but I wonder whether it is precisely that which lies at the heart of real learning.

6 I may seem to be hard on teachers and education, but I am trying to show that whatever their motives and ideas, they are working within an institutionalized understanding of what learning is about. That being so, there is not a lot they can do about it.

7 The idea of learning based on play was in the mind of John Locke when he wrote *Some Thoughts Concerning Education*: 'I have always had a Fancy that Learning might be made a Play and Recreation to Children.' He suggested using a ball with 25 sides [sic] and pasting letters on each side as an example of a game by which children would recognize the English alphabet, for example (*Educational Writings*, CUP, 1968, pp. 255–260). (Source: H. Cunningham, *The Invention of Childhood*, BBC, 2006, p. 112.)

8 Peter and Iona Opie, *The Lore and Language of Schoolchildren*, OUP, 1959.

9 R. Dawkins, *The God Delusion*, Bantam, 2006, p. 31: '… jealous and proud of it; a petty, unjust, unforgiving control freak' but no hint of playfulness or creativity.

10 Hample and Marshall, op. cit.

11 J. Berryman, op. cit., pp. 133–135.

12 R.S. Thomas, *Collected Poems 1945–1990*, Phoenix, 2000.

13 A fine example, possibly the greatest, is Marcel Proust's vast novel, *A La Recherche du Temps Perdu*.

14 For those wanting to explore the five senses further, I commend the work of Maria Montessori and Sofia Cavaletti. If we reflect on family, school and church in the light of these senses, we will discover untapped resources. The Eucharist or Holy Communion speaks to all the senses, for example, just like a family meal. The work of Jerome Berryman on Godly Play is based on rich insights into many ways in which children discover and experience their inner and outer worlds. There is also an excellent section on the five senses in Kristin Herzog, op. cit., pp. 129–134.

15 In my view, we lack a coherent philosophy that allows us to let these two world views converse with each other (shades of Alasdair MacIntyre's *After Virtue*?).

16 I have often heard children talk about when they 'used to do things', and I have known that actually it was a one-off occurrence. The significance of this for me is that something that happens on one occasion may be of unforgettable importance to a child. It can last and affect a lifetime.

17 Geoffrey Best, *Shaftesbury*, Batsford, 1964, p. 30.

18 In one church I know, there seem to be only three songs for children, including 'My God is a great big God', which reminds us week in week out that God is higher than a skyscraper and deeper than a submarine. Can we find no more imaginative and resonating images than these in the whole of the universe?

19 Where are the children's choirs in churches that perform like this? In choir schools, perhaps, but rarely elsewhere. Where are the plays, and where are the orchestras where children and young people can praise God through the music of Bach and others?

20 Margery Williams, *The Velveteen Rabbit*, Egmont, 2004.

Chapter Eight: Hands together

1 In the second edition of *Building the Bonds of Attachment*, Dan Hughes stresses the importance of knowing the life-story and 'baggage' of potential foster carers for the same reason.

2 Dr Jo-Joy Wright, *A Model of Ways of Assessing and Addressing Workers' Needs, using the Framework of White's Key Theologically and Childcare Practice-based Basic Needs of Children (and Adults)*. A summary of this paper is as follows:

Security:
- Clear structures of supervision and support
- Comprehensive systematic assessment at all levels
- Clear job description
- Clear task definition
- Clear contact
- Specified financial budgeting and legitimate expenses
- Basic physical needs met related to work and personal needs

Boundaries:
- Clear documentation
- Clear lines of responsibility and accountability
- Transparent disciplining procedures
- Defined and communicated management structure

Significance:
- Ways for workers' voices to be heard and their ideas honoured
- Affirmation at all levels, especially by the leaders
- Teamwork
- Person-centred, not process-driven
- Valuing people as they are

Community:
- Encourage integration with the local community
- Encouragement for workers to link with communities at home and abroad
- Encourage workers to look beyond their worlds

Creativity:
- Opportunities for training and personal development
- Provide ways in which workers' personal gifts can be heard, valued and exercised
- Stimulate workers' own personal development, spiritually and practically
- Flexibility and adaptability

3 One of the best-known 'wounded healers' in recent times is Henri Nouwen.

Chapter Nine: Hands apart

1 What I want to say about liberal democracy is set in a context where people like Francis Fukuyama have argued that its world-wide acceptance marks 'the end of history'. There are those who see it as the apex or culmination of civilized history. I am more sceptical.

2 This is well described by Jonathan Sacks in *The Politics of Hope*, Jonathan Cape, 1997.

3 One of the intentions of the invasion of Iraq in 2003 was that Iraq might become a beacon of democracy in the Middle East. History will decide whether democracy takes root in Iraq, let alone spreads.

4 In Chapter Two I summarized the work of James Loder. He sets the notion of cognitive and social development in a wider theological setting where the little and great infinities form the ultimate borders of life, and where grace is the link between the two. Cognitive development in this context is going round in circles: it is making progress in its own terms, but it tells us nothing about whether children are closer to or farther from these infinities and grace.

5 Hay and Nye, op. cit., p. 21.

6 For boys, the sale of football shirts with the names of celebrities on them is perhaps one of the most ubiquitous forms of this

kind of marketing. For girls, it is glossy magazines such as *Bliss*.

7 I have given my considered views on this 'The Social Significance of Marriage' (op. cit.). Nothing has changed my views since I wrote it.

8 Sue Palmer, *Toxic Childhood*, Orion, 2006.

Chapter Ten: Villages and compost heaps

1 Other books offer definitions of love, the most accessible being *The Four Loves* by C.S. Lewis (Fount, 2002). There is affection (*storge*), which includes the basic connections between parents and children, with a mixture of gift- and need-love. Then there is friendship (*philia*), which includes 'brotherly' and 'sisterly' love. *Eros* describes what we think of as being 'in love' and includes a sexual dimension. *Agape* is the word used in the phrase 'God is love' (1 John 4:16) and is perhaps best translated as gift-love. The Latin is *caritas*, which gives us the English word 'charity'.

2 I am also following in the tradition of one of my mentors in sociology, Max Weber, who left the 'sociology of religion' undefined right through his major tomes on the subject.

3 In the same way, for an organization to thrive there must be an agreed 'organization in the mind' of its members.

4 I have seen the paper on which a member of the Hitler youth movement pledged his complete loyalty to the Führer: it was a life-or-death matter. That sort of commitment is rare today. Perhaps suicide bombers would say that this is what their commitment is about, but by definition their pledge is time-specific.

5 One of the problems with this idea was that the proposed communities were too small. I was not surprised by this finding: I have in mind an area in which a mother pushing a buggy can reach each boundary within about ten or fifteen minutes of walking.

✶

ACKNOWLEDGMENTS

As you might expect from a book that has been over 20 years in the making, I owe a debt of gratitude to more people and institutions than I can remember.

I am grateful first of all to my own personal family, with whom and through whom I have experienced so much of the meaning and dynamics of love. My parents were committed to the family and community of Mill Grove throughout their lives. It was from them and during the time that they assumed responsibility for Mill Grove that I was able to trace so many of the ways in which love was facilitated and encouraged to grow.

As you will have gathered from the text, it is from the lives of children and their children at Mill Grove that I have derived much of the material for this book. Many of them started out in life in the least promising of circumstances, some suffering neglect, separation, false hopes and abuse. I have seen in them, as individuals and as a community, resilience that has refused to close the doors to love.

In many cases, as an instinctive defence mechanism, they tended to freeze parts of themselves and their past in order to prevent the associations with, and a recurrence of the pain of, separation and loss. But for love to grow there has to be a thaw. If you can recall having frozen fingers during very cold weather and then warming them up by putting them on radiators, you will know that it is an excruciating experience when feeling is resumed. That is a reminder of the cost of the growth of love.

The concern of these children in adulthood for people not related to them by blood over a lifetime and across the world is a remarkable manifestation of love. Although I do not believe that we can explain adequately how love grows, and certainly no one can take the credit for it, it has been my privilege to witness its reality.

In addition to the writers that I mention in the Introduction, there have been many colleagues with whom I have discussed the substance of this book. Diana Richards, a child psychotherapist, for example, supervised my clinical work at Mill Grove for over 15 years, and she has continuously drawn my attention to the fact of love in our midst at Mill Grove, and helped me be more attuned to what is happening.

Dr Jo-Joy Wright, a child psychologist, colleague and friend, has taken up the framework I offer here and reimagined it in her typically creative way.

Michael Reeves, my son-in-law, who is a child psychotherapist, provided insightful comments on the draft text, as well as introducing me to the work of Dan Hughes. Mark Ingham has engaged in a running conversation with me about the five themes from his experience as a head teacher.

I am grateful to students and professional colleagues who have studied and challenged the framework of this book in their own contexts and cultures. I thank colleagues in the National Council of Voluntary Child Care Organizations, the Christian Child Care Forum, the Scottish Institute for Residential Child Care, Bangor University, Royal Holloway University, Spurgeon's College and many other places of higher education on five continents for opportunities to develop the theoretical framework of this book in the context of contemporary experience.

Thanks to Sue Doggett and Lisa Cherrett at BRF for their enthusiasm, encouragement and assistance in the preparation of the manuscript.

And finally, thanks to Sir Richard Bowlby who has commented helpfully on the text, as well as contributing the foreword. It is so appropriate that a book that owes so much to Dr John Bowlby should be introduced by his son.

INDEX

Biblical references